TESLA'S CODE:

MASTERING ENERGY, FREQUENCY, AND CREATIVE POWER

Dr. Constance Santego
Maximillian Enterprises
Kelowna, BC

Copy Editor & Interior Design: Dr. Constance Santego
Book Layout: ©2017 BookDesignTemplates.com
Ordering Information:
Quantity sales. Special discounts are available on quantity purchases by corporations, associations, and others. For details, contact the email below (addressed: "Special Sales Department").

Trade Paperback ISBN: 978-1-990062-45-2
eBook ISBN: 978-1-990062-46-9
Created and published In Canada. Printed and bound in the United States of America

First Edition
Published by Maximillian Enterprises
Kelowna, BC
Canada
www. maximilliane.com
staff@maximilliane.com

*D*edicated to the
pioneers of energy,
frequency, and creative
power—the visionary
thinkers, inventors, and
healers who, inspired by
Nikola Tesla, have dared to
push the boundaries of
science and healing. Your
unwavering commitment to
exploring the unseen forces
that shape our world
continues to light the way
toward a future where
energy, creativity, and
medicine converge for the
greater good of humanity.

ALSO BY DR. CONSTANCE SANTEGO

FICTION
The Nine Spiritual Gifts Series:
Journey of a Soul – (Vol 1 Michael)
Language of a Soul – (Vol 2 Gabriel)
Prophecy of a Soul – (Vol 3 Bath Kol)
Healing of a Soul – (Vol 4 Raphael)
Miracles of a Soul – (Vol 5 Hamied)
Knowledge of a Soul – (Vol 6 Raziel)

NONFICTION
The Intuitive Life, The Gift of Prophecy, Third Edition
Fairy Tales, Dreams and Reality… Where Are You On Your
Path? Second Edition
Your Persona… The Mask You Wear
Angelic Lifestyle, A Vibrant Lifestyle
Angelic Lifestyle 42-Day Energy Cleanse
Archangel Michael's Soul Retrieval Guide
Tesla and the Future of Energy Medicine
Beyond Tesla: Advancing the Science of Energy Healing
Scaling Beyond 6 Figures: *Strategies for Health & Wellness
Professionals*
Beyond the Mind: *Harnessing the Power of Astral Projection for
Creative Awakening*
Bend, Don't Break: *Finding Your Way Back to Abundance*
Ring Therapy: *A Guide to Healing and Balance*
Ring Therapy Pocket Guide
Floraopathy™: *The Art and Science of Vibrational Healing with
Essential Oils*

SECRETS OF A HEALER, SERIES:

Magic Of Aromatherapy (Vol I)
Magic Of Reflexology (Vol II)
Magic Of The Gifts (Vol III)
Magic Of Muscle Testing (Vol IV)
Magic Of Iridology (Vol V)
Magic Of Massage (Vol VI)
Magic Of Hypnotherapy (Vol VII)
Magic Of Reiki (Vol VIII)
Magic Of Advanced Aromatherapy (Vol IX)
Magic Of Esthetics (Vol X)
The Reiki Master's Manual (Vol XI)

ADULT COLORING JOURNALS

SERIES - ZEN COLORING:
Quantum Energy and Mindful Living Journal (Vol 1)
Reiki Energy Journal (Vol 2)
Nine Spiritual Gifts Journal (Vol 3)
I Forgive Journal (Vol 4)

SERIES – COLORING PROSPERITY:
Genie-Inspired Mandalas and Wealth Journal (Vol 1)
Entrepreneurial Mindset Reboot (Vol 2)

SERIES – HARMONIC MIND CODE:
Harmonic Mind Code Coloring Journal (Vol 1)

FOR CHILDREN

I am Big Tonight. I Don't Need the Light!

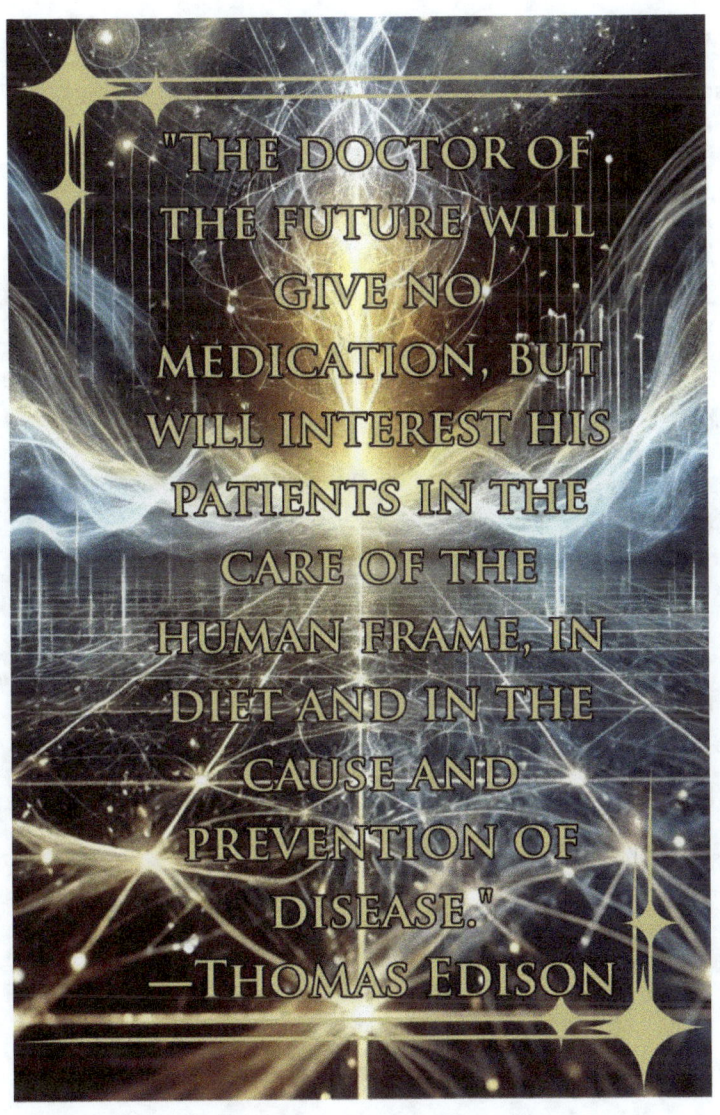

"THE DOCTOR OF THE FUTURE WILL GIVE NO MEDICATION, BUT WILL INTEREST HIS PATIENTS IN THE CARE OF THE HUMAN FRAME, IN DIET AND IN THE CAUSE AND PREVENTION OF DISEASE."
—THOMAS EDISON

Contents

"Medicine repairs the body. Healing awakens the soul. Energy Medicine does both."
—Rhys Thomas

Foreword

The journey that began with *Tesla and the Future of Energy Medicine* introduced readers to the revolutionary ideas of Nikola Tesla—ideas that redefined the way we understand energy, frequency, and vibration in the context of health and healing. In *Beyond Tesla: Advancing the Science of Energy Healing*, we expanded on these theories by exploring the convergence of modern science with ancient wisdom, uncovering new advancements in energy medicine and their potential to transform healthcare as we know it.

Now, with *Tesla's Code: Mastering Energy, Frequency, and Creative Power*, we enter the next phase of this journey—one that invites us to move beyond theory and into practice. This book is designed to take the complex concepts Tesla envisioned and provide readers with the tools to apply them in their own lives. Tesla believed that if we could understand the energetic fabric of the universe, we could unlock limitless potential, both for healing and for creating new realities.

This volume is not just about studying Tesla's work; it is about embodying his principles. It's about mastering the use of energy and frequency to bring balance, health, and creative power into everyday life. Whether you are a healer, an innovator, or simply someone seeking personal growth, the practices outlined in this book will guide you toward a deeper understanding of energy medicine—and a more profound connection to the universe's vibrational nature.

Tesla's legacy is one of innovation, imagination, and an unwavering belief in the potential of the human mind to tap into the unseen forces that govern life itself. This book builds on that legacy, offering readers practical applications for harnessing energy and frequency in ways that can bring about real change in their health, well-being, and creative pursuits.

As you explore *Tesla's Code*, be open to the possibilities that arise. This book is a guide, but it is also an invitation—to experiment, to engage, and to evolve. Through these pages, you will discover that the power to transform your life is not found in the external world but in the mastery of energy, frequency, and the creative forces within you.

Welcome to the next chapter in Tesla's enduring vision—one that is not only about advancing the science of energy healing but about awakening the creative power that lies within us all.

Preface

Nikola Tesla once said, "If you want to find the secrets of the universe, think in terms of energy, frequency, and vibration." In this simple yet profound statement lies the key to not only understanding the universe but also unlocking the potential within ourselves. Over the course of our journey through *Tesla and the Future of Energy Medicine* and *Beyond Tesla: Advancing the Science of Energy Healing*, we have explored how Tesla's pioneering work in electromagnetism and energy has laid the foundation for a new era of healing and scientific discovery. We've delved into the integration of Tesla's principles with modern technology and medicine, illustrating how his vision is shaping the future of healthcare.

Now, in *Tesla's Code: Mastering Energy, Frequency, and Creative Power*, we take a significant step further. This book is designed not just to inform but to empower. It is a guide to mastering the forces that Tesla dedicated his life to understanding—energy, frequency, and vibration—and applying them in your personal and professional life. Tesla believed that these forces were not just the foundation of physical phenomena but also the driving power behind creativity, healing, and transformation.

In this third volume, we will go beyond theory and exploration. We will delve deeply into the practical application of Tesla's discoveries in everyday life. How can we harness energy to improve our health, elevate our consciousness, and unlock our creative potential?

xviii | DR. CONSTANCE SANTEGO

How do frequency and vibration impact not only our physical well-being but also our mental and spiritual growth? This book offers a hands-on approach to integrating Tesla's principles into your daily practices, offering tools, techniques, and exercises to cultivate your inner energy, enhance your creative power, and align yourself with the frequencies that promote healing and transformation.

Tesla was a man ahead of his time, and much of what he envisioned is only now beginning to be realized. *Tesla's Code* represents the culmination of Tesla's life's work, bringing together his discoveries with the emerging science of energy healing and personal mastery. By learning to control and direct energy and frequency, we can unlock deeper layers of human potential, achieve higher levels of creativity, and facilitate profound healing—not just on the physical level but on mental, emotional, and spiritual levels as well.

Whether you are an energy healer, a scientist, a creative professional, or someone on a journey of personal growth, this book is meant to serve as a guide to understanding and mastering the energetic forces that shape your life. The exercises, case studies, and insights presented here are designed to help you embody Tesla's principles, transforming them from abstract concepts into living, practical wisdom.

In the pages ahead, you will discover how to harness the power of your inner energy, align with the frequencies that support your highest potential, and unlock the creative forces within you that Tesla himself believed were the key to all human advancement. As we explore the possibilities that energy and frequency offer for personal transformation, it becomes clear that Tesla's legacy is more relevant than ever before.

Join me as we unlock the secrets of energy, frequency, and vibration—three fundamental forces that have the potential to change not only how we understand the universe but also how we live our lives. The future Tesla envisioned is now within reach, and the journey to mastering *Tesla's Code* begins here.

With gratitude and inspiration, Dr. Constance Santego

Note to Reader

*D*ear Reader,

Welcome to *Tesla's Code: Mastering Energy, Frequency, and Creative Power*. This book is the next step in our shared journey, following *Tesla and the Future of Energy Medicine* and *Beyond Tesla: Advancing the Science of Energy Healing*. In this volume, we dive into the practical applications of Nikola Tesla's revolutionary principles—energy, frequency, and vibration—and explore how they can be harnessed to unlock your inner potential and transform your life.

This book is about taking what we've learned from Tesla's visionary work and modern advancements in energy healing and applying those insights to empower you on a personal and energetic level. As you embark on this new journey, I offer a few thoughts to enhance your experience:

1. **Harness the Power of Energy**: In *Tesla's Code*, you'll explore Tesla's principles through a practical lens. This book is designed to help you *apply* the concepts of energy, frequency, and vibration in your everyday life. Whether you're looking to enhance your health, creativity, or spiritual growth, the exercises and insights in these chapters are meant to offer hands-on tools that empower you to master your own energy.

2. **A Practical Guide for Personal Transformation**: Unlike the previous volumes that focused on the theoretical and scientific underpinnings of energy medicine, this book emphasizes *practical application*. Each chapter is designed to guide you through exercises, visualizations, and techniques that will help you activate your inner energy and align with the frequencies that promote healing and creative power.

3. **Accessible to All**: Whether you are a seasoned energy practitioner or someone new to the concepts of energy healing, this book offers something for everyone. The techniques in *Tesla's Code* are broken down in a way that makes them accessible, no matter your experience level. It's not just about advanced knowledge but also about cultivating a daily practice that resonates with your life and goals.

4. **Engage with Your Own Energy Field**: This book is an invitation to explore and engage with your energy field on a personal level. Reflective exercises, visualization practices, and affirmations throughout the chapters are included to help you connect with your energy, align your vibration, and unlock your creative potential.

5. **Ongoing Learning and Expansion**: While this book focuses on applying Tesla's principles, it also provides opportunities to expand your understanding of the science and philosophy behind energy healing. As you practice and explore these concepts, I encourage you to revisit earlier works or explore the additional resources and case studies provided at the end to deepen your knowledge.

6. **Be an Active Participant**: Your experience with *Tesla's Code* is not meant to be passive.

It's about *active engagement*—applying techniques, experimenting with frequency, and tapping into your creative energy. Join the community of like-minded individuals who are also exploring these concepts, whether through online platforms, workshops, or discussions. Share your experiences and insights, as we are all learning together in this evolving field.

This book is a culmination of the principles that Tesla pioneered, now being brought into everyday life to promote personal transformation and empowerment. It offers not only a deep understanding of energy, frequency, and vibration but also the tools to master them. My hope is that this book inspires you to take charge of your energy, awaken your creative potential, and embrace the power that lies within you.

Thank you for embarking on this transformative journey with me. May this book guide you toward mastering the extraordinary creative power of energy and frequency in your life.

With great anticipation and respect,

Dr. Constance Santego

Learning Outcome

Upon completing *Tesla's Code: Mastering Energy, Frequency, and Creative Power*, readers will:

1. **Deepen Their Understanding of Tesla's Vision on Energy and Frequency:**
   - o **Explore Tesla's Insights**: Gain a comprehensive understanding of how Tesla's revolutionary ideas on energy, frequency, and vibration continue to shape modern concepts of healing and creative power.
2. **Master the Principles of Inner Energy and Vibrational Healing:**
   - o **Inner Mastery**: Learn advanced techniques for accessing and harnessing inner energy (chi), developing a profound connection with personal and universal energy fields to promote healing and transformation.
3. **Integrate Energy, Frequency, and Creativity for Holistic Healing:**
   - o **Holistic Application**: Discover how to integrate the principles of energy and frequency with creative visualization, sound healing, and Tesla's methods to unlock personal power and enhance physical, emotional, and spiritual well-being.
4. **Implement Practical Techniques for Energy Healing and Personal Growth:**

○ **Practical Empowerment**: Gain practical skills in applying vibrational healing techniques in everyday life, from enhancing vitality through energy work to manifesting intentions through creative power.

5. **Develop the Ability to Harness Creative Power for Transformation:**
    ○ **Creative Manifestation**: Understand the science and metaphysics behind using energy and frequency to manifest desired outcomes, tapping into Tesla's methods of visualization and intention to influence reality and foster personal transformation.

6. **Analyze Advanced Healing Modalities Rooted in Tesla's Teachings:**
    ○ **Innovation and Tradition**: Investigate modern healing modalities inspired by Tesla's discoveries, including sound healing, scalar energy, and quantum field applications, and how they can be adapted for personal and professional use.

7. **Foster a Deeper Connection to Consciousness and Universal Energy:**
    ○ **Consciousness Expansion**: Explore the relationship between energy, consciousness, healing, and how aligning with universal energy principles can enhance intuitive abilities and spiritual growth.

8. **Shape the Future of Energy Healing through Personal Mastery:**
    ○ **Visionary Leadership**: Cultivate the skills to lead in the field of energy healing by mastering Tesla's principles of frequency, vibration, and creative

power, applying them to both personal development and the broader realm of energy medicine.

Conclusion: This book equips readers with a deep, practical, and advanced understanding of Tesla's principles of energy, frequency, and creative power. Through mastery of inner energy and vibrational healing, readers will be empowered to transform their lives, foster personal and spiritual growth, and contribute to the future of energy medicine and holistic healing.

Chapter 1

Introduction to Tesla's Code

Energy as a Universal Force

Energy is the foundation of everything we do—whether it's the movement of our bodies or the way we communicate over vast distances. Nikola Tesla's pioneering work revealed that energy is not merely a spiritual or abstract concept but a real, tangible force that governs the universe.

Tesla understood that everything in existence vibrates at a specific frequency, from human thoughts and emotions to the physical world around us. His groundbreaking insights into energy transmission demonstrated that energy flows through invisible waves, much like how a cell phone transmits signals across space. Whether it's through electrical currents, radio waves, or vibrational frequencies, Tesla's discoveries show us that energy is the unseen force connecting and powering the world around us.

Tesla's Vision and Perception

Imagine perception—much like tuning into a radio frequency—picking up on subtle vibrations all around us. Just as a phone call transmits signals across space, this perception allows us to sense and decode the unseen energies that surround us. Nikola Tesla, in his work with electromagnetic waves, demonstrated how energy can be transmitted wirelessly across long distances, and in a similar way, our perceptive ability tunes into the energies of people, places, and events. While we can't see these energy waves, they are real, powerful, and constantly in motion.

Tesla's legacy offers a scientific framework for understanding how energy—both physical and perceptual—moves and interacts with the world. By learning to tune into specific frequencies, just as Tesla did with wireless energy, we can influence and manipulate these forces. This heightened perception allows us to interpret and respond to the energetic vibrations around us, much like Tesla's ability to read and harness the natural energies of the universe.

Energy and Sensory Perception

In quantum physics, energy is understood as the driving force behind the interactions between particles and fields. When it comes to sensory perception—the ability to "sense" or "read" energy—it can be likened to the process of decoding vibrational frequencies. This is similar to how electromagnetic signals are translated into information, where energy patterns are interpreted as data, sound, or imagery.

Tesla's pioneering work on energy transmission, particularly in alternating current (AC) and wireless communication, provides a useful framework for understanding how energy moves through space. His insights reveal that energy in its various forms travels at incredible speeds—sometimes even faster than light when considering the non-local effects seen in quantum systems. This closely aligns with sensory perception, which often feels instantaneous, transcending the conventional limits of time and space. Intuition functions like quantum energy transfer, where information is sensed, received, and interpreted rapidly, often beyond conscious awareness.

By applying Tesla's principles of energy and frequency, we gain valuable insights into how we can learn to sense and perceive these subtle energy fields. Tesla's ability to mentally simulate and detect energy flows can be translated into practical techniques that allow us to tune into the vibrations around us—whether from people, objects, or the environment. Developing this intuitive perception enables us to "read" these energetic frequencies with greater precision and sensitivity, helping us attune to the unseen forces that shape our world.

Introduction to Sensory Perception and Intuition

Sensory perception is often thought of in terms of the traditional five senses: sight, hearing, touch, taste, and smell. These senses allow us to experience and interpret the physical world around us by processing information received through external stimuli. However, modern science, particularly in fields like quantum physics and neuroscience, suggests that perception extends beyond these physical senses into more subtle realms of experience—what many refer to as intuition.

Intuition, often described as a "sixth sense," is the ability to perceive or understand things without the need for conscious reasoning. From a scientific standpoint, intuition can be thought of as the brain's ability to process information rapidly, drawing from patterns, past experiences, and subconscious cues to provide insights or "gut feelings." Though these signals may bypass logical analysis, they are often informed by subtle sensory inputs and accumulated knowledge that the conscious mind may not immediately recognize.

In the realm of quantum mechanics, the idea of perceiving subtle energy fields and vibrations aligns with the understanding that everything in the universe vibrates at specific frequencies. Nikola Tesla's work on energy transmission, particularly through wireless technology and alternating current (AC), offers a scientific foundation for understanding how energy moves in invisible waves. This transmission of energy is not limited to electrical systems—it is a universal phenomenon that extends to the vibrational nature of human thoughts, emotions, and interactions.

The Science of Intuitive Perception

Intuitive perception is not mystical but rather a reflection of the brain's ability to tap into subtle environmental cues. Neuroscientists have shown that the brain continuously gathers vast amounts of data from both internal and external environments. Some of this data is processed consciously, but a significant portion is handled at the subconscious level, where it may influence decisions, insights, and emotional responses without our immediate awareness.

Furthermore, quantum physics suggests that at the most fundamental level, we are all interconnected through energy fields that operate beyond the constraints of time and space. This concept of non-locality—where particles can influence each other instantaneously over large distances—parallels the notion that our minds and senses may also be capable of perceiving information that transcends physical limitations.

Tesla's insights into energy as a universal force show us that just as energy can be transmitted wirelessly, perceptual awareness may operate similarly. Subtle vibrational signals—whether emotional, mental, or environmental—are constantly being transmitted and received. Intuition can, therefore, be understood as a kind of sensory perception that processes these vibrations, allowing us to "read" energies or sense shifts in our surroundings.

Developing Intuitive Perception Through Sensory Awareness

The good news is that intuitive perception can be cultivated and refined, much like any of the five physical senses. Tesla's visionary understanding of energy and frequency provides a scientific framework for exploring how we can train ourselves to tune into vibrational frequencies that go unnoticed by our conscious minds.

By learning to recognize and trust the subtle signals our minds receive—whether from physical spaces, people, or situations—we can enhance our ability to make insightful decisions and explore creative solutions. Sensory perception and intuition are not separate phenomena; rather, they are part of a spectrum of awareness that extends from the physical to the vibrational, ultimately helping us navigate both the seen and unseen aspects of reality.

Exercise #1:
Complimentary Colors Visualization

In Tesla's method of visualizing inventions, he held images with incredible clarity and vividness. This mental practice of detailed visualization is something anyone can develop. Just as Tesla focused on every element of his inventions, from the smallest mechanical part to the energy flows between components, you can train your mind to sharpen its visual focus using color.

Purpose: The Complimentary Colors Visualization exercise will help you enhance mental clarity, improve focus, and train your brain to hold vivid images. This is the same mental strength Tesla used to perfect his inventions before they ever reached the physical world.

Instructions:

1. Find a quiet place where you can sit comfortably without distractions.
2. Close your eyes and begin to focus on your breathing. Inhale deeply and exhale slowly, allowing your mind to relax.
3. Visualize a specific color in your mind's eye. It could be a primary color like blue, red, or yellow. Focus on holding this color in your mental field.
4. Now, think of its complimentary color. If you visualized blue, switch to orange. If you start with red, transition to green, and if yellow, move to purple.
5. Switch back and forth between the original color and its complimentary shade. Notice any shifts in brightness or intensity as you visualize these hues.
6. Increase the detail: Imagine these colors on objects, such as a vibrant red apple or the green leaves of a tree. Focus on texture, light reflection, and any shadows that form.

7. Repeat this process for 5 to 10 minutes, gradually adding more complexity to your visualizations. Challenge yourself to visualize multiple objects or settings, just as Tesla would hold an entire machine in his mind.

Goal: By regularly practicing this exercise, you will strengthen your ability to hold vivid, detailed mental images. This skill will become invaluable as you proceed through the exercises in this book, learning to visualize complex ideas, energy flows, and outcomes with Tesla-like precision.

Chapter 2

Light Energy: A Deeper Understanding

To grasp Tesla's Code, it's essential to first understand the nature of energy. In its simplest form, energy is the ability to cause movement or change. But what exactly is energy? The dictionary offers several definitions, including:

- Forcefulness and vigor in actions or words
- Busy activity, such as devoting one's energy to an endeavor
- In physics, energy is a unifying concept in all systems, manifesting as kinetic energy (from motion), potential energy (from position), or radiant energy (from photons).

The most famous equation related to energy is Einstein's $E=mc^2$, which highlights the relationship between mass and energy. This formula reveals that even an object at rest contains a tremendous amount of energy. Essentially, energy is everywhere, powering all movement and change in the universe.

- Did you know there are many forms of energy? These include Magnetic, Electrical, Sound, Gravitational, Elastic, Light, Thermal, Mechanical, Chemical, and Nuclear energy. These types can be grouped into three categories:

- Potential Energy – Stored energy related to an object's position, such as Elastic, Nuclear, and Chemical energy.
- Kinetic Energy – Energy of motion, including Mechanical, Thermal, and Sound energy.
- Radiant Energy – Energy that exists without particles, like Light and Intuition.

In *Tesla's Code*, the focus is on **vibrational energy**—a form of energy that operates beyond the realm of physical particles, much like intuition or extrasensory perception (ESP). Just as ultraviolet and infrared light are invisible to the human eye, certain energies exist outside the scope of our typical senses. It is within this subtle realm that Tesla's principles of energy and frequency take on profound relevance.

Consider that telephones, airplanes, and moon landings were once unimaginable. Today, they are part of everyday life. In the same way, intuition or ESP—once viewed as mystical or unprovable—may soon be understood as a **form of energy**, perhaps even a type of light energy.

Tesla's work in wireless energy transmission offers clues to this possibility. Just as electrical energy can be transmitted without wires, it's plausible that intuition operates through **unseen energy fields**. The idea that intuition is a form of light energy may not be as far-fetched as it once seemed. In fact, scientists studying subatomic particles, like quarks, are uncovering new possibilities in the nature of energy and consciousness.

In this book, you'll discover how to harness light energy, even if it remains beyond your direct perception. Just as radio waves or light waves outside the visible spectrum exist unseen, intuition and other subtle forms of energy operate beyond our physical senses. By applying Tesla's principles of energy and frequency, we can begin to engage with these hidden forces to enhance our well-being and deepen our understanding of the world around us.

The future of energy rests in our capacity to comprehend and manipulate it in ways that are yet to be fully uncovered. It's entirely plausible that intuition itself is a form of light energy—radiating within and around us, waiting to be accessed for insight, creativity, and deeper awareness.

Chapter 3

Vibration, Frequency & Life Force Energy

Grasping the science of vibration and frequency is essential for understanding and harnessing **life force energy**, which Tesla regarded as a core element of the universe. These principles form the basis of both the physical world and the invisible forces that shape it. To access and strengthen your connection with this life force energy, you must raise your vibrational frequency, aligning it with higher energetic states.

Tesla's work with energy transmission and frequency demonstrates that **vibration** is not just a physical phenomenon but a universal principle governing both matter and consciousness. By tuning into these frequencies, Tesla believed we could unlock new ways to access power, heal, and even expand our awareness.

Vibration Defined

- **Vibration** refers to the periodic motion of particles within an elastic body or medium, oscillating back and forth from a point of equilibrium when disturbed. This concept is present in everything from the strings of a musical instrument to the transmission of sound waves through air.
- Vibration also describes an **energetic field** or **aura** that emanates from all living and non-living things, creating a distinct vibratory signature. This

energy can be **felt** or **instinctively sensed**, though it is often invisible to the eye.

Frequency Defined

- Frequency is the rate at which a repeating event occurs, typically measured in **hertz (Hz).** One hertz represents one cycle per second.
- In physical terms, frequency plays a crucial role in various natural phenomena. For example, sound waves consist of oscillating pressure, and their frequency determines the pitch we hear. While humans can detect sound between 20 Hz and 16,000 Hz, frequencies beyond this range—like ultrasound or infrasound—exist at molecular and atomic levels, even though we cannot perceive them.

Frequency and the Universe

Frequency governs the formation of everything in the universe. It allows energy to manifest in various forms, from particles and atoms to stars, planets, and biological life. Each object, whether living or non-living, has its own unique **vibrational signature**.

For example, **a solid metal chair** feels rigid because its molecules vibrate slowly and are tightly packed together. On the other hand, **air molecules** vibrate quickly and are far apart, making air invisible and fluid.

The human body is made up of trillions of cells, each vibrating at its own frequency. While we can't perceive these microscopic vibrations, they are measurable. Scientists like **Dr. Valerie Hunt** have shown that the human body maintains a healthy frequency between 62-78 MHz. Illness, such as cancer, lowers this frequency, but by raising the body's vibration, healing can be facilitated.

Resonance and Vibrational Alignment

An important concept in frequency is **resonance**—the phenomenon where one vibrating system influences another to vibrate at the same frequency. This principle can be seen in everything from musical instruments to human relationships. When two people's energy fields resonate, they feel more connected, just as harmonious frequencies create music. Tesla believed that by tuning into the **right frequencies**, we could better understand both the physical and metaphysical realms of life force energy.

Hertz: The Measurement of Frequency

- **Hertz (Hz)** measures the frequency in cycles per second, much like inches or centimeters measure distance.
- Named after **Heinrich Rudolf Hertz**, who demonstrated the existence of electromagnetic waves, hertz is an important unit when discussing the rate of vibrations, particularly those under 1,000 cycles per second.

Exercise #2:
Aura Visualization for Tapping into Vibrational Energy

Tesla believed that everything, both living and non-living, vibrates with a distinct energy frequency. Just as objects emit vibrational frequencies, so do our thoughts, ideas, and intentions. This exercise will help you sense the aura—or energy field—of your projects, challenges, or even yourself. By developing the ability to visualize and perceive this energy, you can refine and align your intentions with higher vibrations.

Purpose: This exercise will help you become attuned to the vibrational frequency surrounding a specific idea or challenge, enabling you to adjust its energy for more effective outcomes.

Instructions:

1. Prepare for the exercise by sitting in a quiet, comfortable place where you can focus. Close your eyes and take a few deep breaths, allowing your body and mind to relax.
2. Visualize an object, idea, or challenge you are working on, much like Tesla would envision his inventions. Picture it clearly in your mind as if it were a solid object in front of you.
3. Sense the aura of your visualization: Now, focus on the energy surrounding this visualization. Imagine a glowing aura around it—what color is it? Is the energy vibrant, or does it feel dull? Allow yourself to instinctively feel the vibrational quality of the aura.
4. Interpret the aura: If the aura feels strong and vibrant, consider what's working well in your approach. If it feels weak or unbalanced, think

about what aspects might need adjustment. Allow this intuitive perception to guide your understanding of the energy behind your project or idea.

5. Adjust the energy: Mentally adjust the aura, brightening its color, expanding its vibrational field, and filling it with positive, higher-frequency energy. Imagine your project or idea becoming more aligned, harmonious, and powerful as you work with its aura.

6. Spend 5-10 minutes visualizing this process. When you feel that the energy is balanced and aligned, gradually bring your awareness back to the present moment.

Goal: This exercise helps you intuitively sense the energy field of your ideas, enabling you to adjust their vibrational alignment for greater resonance and success. By learning to perceive and refine these energetic auras, you can elevate the vibrational frequency of both yourself and your projects, much like Tesla aligned his ideas with universal forces.

Exercise #3 Practical Application: Tapping into Higher Vibrations

To raise your rate and connect with life force energy, you can start by incorporating practices that align with higher frequencies:

- **Breathing exercises:** Conscious deep breathing can elevate your energy by oxygenating your cells and calming your mind.
- **Meditation and visualization:** These practices help attune your mind to subtle energy fields and higher frequencies.
- **Resonance awareness:** Be mindful of the energy you surround yourself with—whether it's people, environments, or even thoughts. By tuning into higher vibrations, you can cultivate a more balanced and energized state of being.

By grasping the principles of vibration and frequency as Tesla did, you start to recognize that vibrational energy is not merely an abstract concept but a tangible force that can be measured, harnessed, and directed to deepen your connection with the world around you.

Chapter 4

Tesla's Concept of Life Force Energy and Visualization as a Creative Tool

Tesla's Concept of Life Force Energy

Nikola Tesla believed that life itself was an expression of energy, with the human body and mind acting as receivers and transmitters of this universal force. He proposed that an underlying "life force" permeates all matter and living beings, akin to ancient concepts like prana, qi, or chi— energies that animate life and connect us to the cosmos.

Tesla's work with energy, especially his experiments in wireless energy transmission, suggested that life force energy operates at a frequency beyond the visible spectrum. This energy is subtle, fast-moving, and exists on a plane that requires heightened awareness and sensitivity to access. Tesla recognized this vibrational energy as crucial to both physical vitality and mental clarity, influencing our health, creativity, and a deeper connection to the universe.

The Three Levels of Tesla's Life Force Energy

In this chapter, we explore three distinct levels of frequency rooted in Tesla's understanding of vibrational energy:

- **Electromagnetic Vibration** – This energy is linked to the Earth's magnetic fields and is essential for regulating the biological functions of the body. The Earth's electromagnetic fields affect everything from our sleep cycles to our overall sense of well-being. Tesla understood that human health is connected to these natural forces, and by aligning with them, we can enhance our physical state.

- **Physical Vibration** – Every object, whether living or non-living, emits vibrational frequencies. These vibrations interact with our energy fields and either harmonize or disrupt our personal energy. From people to machines, physical vibration influences us more than we often realize. Tesla knew that by managing these external vibrations, we could better balance our internal energy fields and maintain emotional and physical equilibrium.

- **Etheric Vibration** – This is where Tesla's concept of life force energy expands. Etheric vibration connects us to the cosmic forces of the universe. This fast-moving, subtle energy operates on a higher plane, beyond the physical senses. Tesla's experiments in wireless energy hinted at the possibility that unseen, yet very real, forces govern much of the universe's power. By tuning into these etheric vibrations, we can access higher knowledge, inspiration, and creativity—just as Tesla did.

By raising your vibrational frequency, you can tap into the life force energy Tesla believed was the key to personal empowerment and a deeper connection with the cosmos. This energy, once harnessed, can unlock creative potential and help solve problems with greater clarity.

Visualization as a Creative Tool

Visualization is more than just seeing images in your mind—it's a practice that engages your inner world to unlock creativity, solve problems, and bring ideas to life. Nikola Tesla, one of the greatest inventors and visionaries of modern times, mastered this practice in extraordinary ways. Tesla didn't rely on traditional models or blueprints to develop his groundbreaking ideas. Instead, he used the power of mental imagery and vibrational alignment to create entire inventions in his mind before ever building them in the physical world.

Tesla's visualization process wasn't abstract or vague; it was detailed, precise, and immersive. He mentally constructed his inventions down to the smallest details, running mental simulations to test their functionality, identify potential issues, and make improvements. He could see his machines working, disassembling, and reassembling them in his mind, and when he finally brought his ideas into reality, they worked exactly as he had envisioned.

In this section, you'll explore how to harness the same power of visualization to enhance your own creativity. Whether you're an inventor, artist, entrepreneur, or someone seeking to solve problems more effectively, visualization can become a powerful tool for bringing your ideas to life. Just as Tesla visualized entire machines and systems, you can train yourself to mentally simulate the steps, processes, and outcomes of your creative endeavors.

How Visualization Unlocks Creativity

Visualization is not just about imagination—it's the bridge between the abstract and the real. When you visualize, your brain engages similarly to how it processes real experiences. Studies have shown that when people visualize an action—whether it's running, designing, or speaking—the brain activates the same regions it would use if they were physically performing that action. This is why visualization is such a powerful tool for creativity and problem-solving.

Tesla used his mind as a workshop. He didn't just imagine how things looked; he visualized how they functioned, how parts moved together, and how energy flowed through them. This allowed him to troubleshoot potential issues before they ever arose in real life, making his process highly creative and efficient.

Through visualization, you can access the same creative power. By mentally exploring concepts, testing different ideas, and experimenting with possibilities, you unlock a world of solutions that might not be immediately obvious. Your inner vision becomes a creative laboratory where you can build, refine, and perfect your ideas without limitations.

The Key Elements of Tesla's Visualization Process

Tesla's method of visualization can be broken down into a few key elements that anyone can learn and apply:

1. **Vivid Mental Imagery** – Tesla's visualizations weren't fleeting thoughts. He could see his inventions in crystal-clear detail. Every nut, bolt, and mechanism appeared to him as if it were physically present. This level of precision allowed him to work with his inventions mentally as if they already existed in the physical world.
2. **Mental Simulation** – Tesla didn't just look at his designs—he mentally operated them. He could visualize how a machine would work in real-time, identifying potential weaknesses and making adjustments entirely within his mind. His mental simulations were so accurate that when the machines were finally built, they functioned almost exactly as he had visualized them.
3. **Refinement and Perfection** – By using his mind to simulate his inventions, Tesla continuously refined and improved his ideas without the need for physical prototypes. He perfected his designs before ever building them, allowing him to skip the traditional trial-and-error process. Visualization allowed him to make mistakes and correct them in the safety of his own mind.

Applying Tesla's Visualization Techniques

Visualization can be applied to almost any area of life—from business ventures and artistic projects to personal goals and problem-solving. Here are a few ways to practice Tesla's visualization techniques:

- **Visualizing an Entire Process** – Pick a project or challenge you're working on and visualize every step from start to finish. Focus on the details, just as Tesla would mentally simulate the functioning of his inventions. See yourself overcoming challenges, making improvements, and completing the task successfully.
- **Mental Simulation for Creative Problem-Solving** – When faced with a problem, use visualization to mentally explore different scenarios and solutions. Run mental simulations to see which path might work best, allowing yourself to adjust and refine your ideas before putting them into action.
- **Refining Ideas Through Mental Practice** – Just as Tesla perfected his inventions through mental practice, you can refine your own ideas. Whether you're working on a creative project or trying to solve a difficult problem, use visualization to explore possibilities, test different approaches, and make improvements until you reach the best solution.

Becoming a Modern-Day Visionary

By adopting Tesla's method of visualization, you can unlock your own creative potential. Visualization is a powerful tool that allows you to see the unseen, imagine the impossible, and make it a reality. Through vivid mental imagery, mental simulations, and constant refinement, you can bring your ideas to life with precision and clarity—just as Tesla did.

In the chapters to come, we will explore how you can use Tesla's visualization techniques not only to create but to innovate, solve problems, and tap into higher frequencies of energy for deeper insight and personal growth.

Chapter 5

Visualizing Innovation Like Tesla

In the previous chapter, we explored Tesla's unique approach to visualization and how he used it to bring his groundbreaking inventions to life. But Tesla's genius wasn't just in creating individual machines—it was in his ability to imagine revolutionary, large-scale systems that transformed the course of human history. Whether it was the alternating current (AC) system that powered the world or his visionary work on wireless energy transmission, Tesla always thought on a grand scale. In this chapter, we'll explore how you can apply the power of visualization to innovate on a large scale, just as Tesla did.

Seeing the Entire Process

When Tesla visualized his inventions, he didn't just see individual components. He saw the entire process—the way energy moved, how parts interacted, and what the final outcome would look like. He didn't stop at envisioning a single device; he thought about how that device would function within a broader system. This holistic approach to visualization allowed him to innovate beyond the invention itself and solve large, systemic problems.

Key Concept: Holistic Visualization

Holistic visualization means seeing the bigger picture, not just the individual parts. To innovate on a large scale, you must mentally visualize how all the elements fit together.

Whether you're building a business, designing a product, or creating a work of art, it's essential to envision the entire process from conception to completion.

Exercise #4:
Project Visualization

1. **Choose a Big Idea:** Pick a project or goal you're currently working on or something you've always dreamed of pursuing.
2. **Visualize the Process:** Close your eyes and imagine the project from start to finish. What are the major steps? What resources will you need? What challenges might arise? Mentally simulate each stage, just as Tesla did with his inventions.
3. **Focus on Interconnections:** Don't just visualize individual tasks—think about how they connect. How do the various parts of your project work together? What needs to happen for everything to come together smoothly?
4. **Note the Details:** As you visualize, pay attention to specific details. What does success look like? How does it feel? Visualize the final outcome in vivid detail.

By regularly practicing holistic visualization, you train your mind to see beyond immediate tasks and start thinking in systems. This ability to zoom out and see the entire process is essential for large-scale innovation.

Mental Simulation for Long-Term Goals

Tesla didn't just visualize short-term projects; he used mental simulations to work through long-term goals and innovations that would take years to fully realize. His work on wireless energy transmission, for example, was a long-term vision that extended far beyond the technological possibilities of his time. Despite the obstacles, he continuously refined and mentally tested his ideas for decades.

Key Concept: Long-Term Thinking

To be a true visionary, you must think beyond the short-term and visualize outcomes that may take years to materialize. This requires patience, persistence, and the ability to foresee potential obstacles far in advance.

Exercise #5:
Long-Term Goal Visualization

1. **Choose a Long-Term Goal**: Think about a goal that may take years to achieve—whether it's building a successful company, completing a large creative project, or making a significant life change.
2. **Visualize the Future:** Mentally project yourself five or ten years into the future. What does your life look like if you've achieved your goal? Visualize the path that got you there. What steps did you take along the way? What challenges did you overcome?
3. **Identify Obstacles:** As you visualize, think about the potential obstacles you might face. How can you prepare for them? What resources or strategies will you need to stay on track?
4. **Refine Your Plan:** Use your visualization to mentally adjust and refine your long-term plan. Are there any changes you can make now to improve your chances of success?
   By regularly visualizing long-term goals, you prepare yourself for future challenges. This helps you stay focused, adapt to obstacles, and maintain a clear vision of your ultimate success.

Visionary Thinking: Pushing Beyond Limits

Tesla was a visionary not simply because he improved on existing ideas but because he pushed the boundaries of what was considered possible. His work on wireless energy, for example, was far ahead of his time, and even though it wasn't fully realized during his life, his groundbreaking ideas laid the foundation for modern technologies like wireless communication and renewable energy systems.

Tesla wasn't afraid to dream big, and he believed that the limits we perceive are often self-imposed. By imagining what's beyond the horizon, he opened up new possibilities for innovation.

Key Concept: Visionary Thinking

Visionary thinking requires pushing beyond the limits of what you know or what seems possible. It's about seeing potential where others see impossibility and daring to imagine solutions that haven't yet been tried.

Exercise #6:
Visionary Innovation

1. **Think Beyond the Present**: Choose a problem or challenge in your life, your work, or the world around you. Instead of thinking about current solutions, ask yourself: What could be possible in 10, 20, or even 50 years?
2. **Visualize Without Limits**: Let go of the limitations of current technology or resources. Imagine the most creative, groundbreaking solution possible. What would it look like? How would it work?
3. **Refine Your Vision:** Once you've imagined the big picture, refine your vision. What are the first steps you can take now to start moving toward this future? What can you do today to push beyond your current limits?

By practicing visionary thinking, you train yourself to see opportunities where others see challenges. This ability to think beyond the present is the key to true innovation.

Visualization Blueprint: Bringing Your Big Ideas to Life

Tesla's ability to mentally construct and refine his inventions allowed him to skip the traditional trial-and-error process and move directly from vision to reality. By creating a mental blueprint of your project or goal, you can bring your big ideas to life with greater clarity and precision.

Key Concept: Visualization Blueprint

A visualization blueprint is a mental map of your project, showing all the steps and connections between them. It's like a mental version of a traditional blueprint but with more flexibility, allowing you to test, refine, and perfect your idea before it becomes real.

Exercise #7:
Create Your Visualization Blueprint

1. **Define Your Idea:** Choose a major project or goal you want to work on—something that feels big and ambitious.
2. **Visualize the Blueprint:** Close your eyes and start visualizing the entire project as a mental blueprint. Imagine all the components, how they fit together, and how they'll work in real life.
3. **Test and Refine**: Mentally simulate each part of the process. Where might problems arise? What improvements can you make? Refine your blueprint as you go along.
4. **Bring It to Life:** Once you've created a detailed mental blueprint, start bringing your idea to life. Begin with small, actionable steps that align with your vision.

By using a visualization blueprint, you can mentally simulate the process of bringing your ideas to life before you ever start building them in the physical world. This allows you to troubleshoot, refine, and perfect your ideas, just as Tesla did with his inventions.

Exercise #8:
Remote Viewing for Project Visualization

Tesla's ability to mentally simulate inventions and see how they would operate in different contexts is akin to the concept of remote viewing, where one visualizes distant or unseen environments. This exercise helps you develop the skill of visualizing your projects from multiple perspectives, much like Tesla did when mentally simulating his large-scale innovations.

Purpose: To train your mind to project itself into future scenarios, enabling you to visualize how your projects or ideas will manifest, overcome obstacles, and function in various environments.

Instructions:

1. **Prepare a Quiet Space:** Find a comfortable, quiet place to focus. Close your eyes and take a few deep breaths to calm your mind and body.
2. **Choose a Project or Goal:** Select a project or long-term goal that you want to visualize in detail. It could be a personal or professional endeavor, much like Tesla visualizing an invention or system.
3. **Visualize Your Current Position:** Begin by visualizing where you are currently with this project. What steps have you taken so far? What obstacles have you faced? Picture your present situation with as much clarity as possible.
4. **Project Forward in Time:** Now, mentally "travel" into the future. Visualize your project one year from now. Where do you see yourself? How has the project evolved? What milestones have

you reached? Picture the steps you've taken to reach this point.

5. **View Multiple Outcomes:** Continue projecting forward to visualize several different possible outcomes for your project. What does success look like? What challenges might you face? Visualize different scenarios and how each might unfold.

6. **Remote Viewing in Different Environments:** Now imagine your project functioning in various contexts. For example, if it's a product, visualize it being used by customers in different settings. If it's a business, see how it operates in different markets. Expand your mind to see how your project impacts the world.

7. **Take Notes:** After completing the exercise, take notes on the insights or visuals that came to you during the remote viewing. How did each outcome feel? What obstacles or opportunities appeared?

Goal: This exercise sharpens your ability to see beyond the present moment and visualize how your project or goal will evolve over time and across different environments. Just as Tesla anticipated the future impact of his inventions, remote viewing helps you gain foresight and clarity about your long-term endeavors.

Becoming a Modern-Day Visionary

Tesla's ability to visualize large-scale innovations changed the world. By applying his methods of holistic visualization, mental simulation, and visionary thinking, you, too, can become a modern-day visionary. Whether your goal is to invent, create, or solve complex problems, visualization is the key to unlocking the power of your mind and turning big ideas into reality.

In the next chapter, we will explore how to channel thought energy—another technique Tesla mastered—to further amplify your creativity and innovation. Just as Tesla believed that thoughts carried their own vibrational power, you will learn how to focus and harness your thoughts to shape the reality around you.

Chapter 6

Harnessing Thought Energy Like Tesla

In previous chapters, we've explored Nikola Tesla's mastery of visualization and how he used mental simulations to bring his inventions to life. However, Tesla's genius extended beyond mental imagery—he believed that thoughts themselves carried vibrational power, capable of shaping and influencing reality. In this chapter, we'll delve into Tesla's concept of thought energy and how you can harness this force to enhance your creativity, manifest your goals, and innovate at a deeper level.

Tesla famously said, "If you want to find the secrets of the universe, think in terms of energy, frequency, and vibration." This belief was not limited to his work in physics and engineering—it formed the basis of how he viewed the power of the mind. He understood that thought energy is a real, tangible force that, when directed with intention, could create remarkable change.

By the end of this chapter, you'll learn how to focus your thoughts with precision, amplify their energy, and use them to manifest your creative ideas, just as Tesla did.

The Power of Thought Energy

Tesla believed that thoughts operate on frequencies, much like radio waves or electrical currents. When we think with clarity and focus, we send out vibrational signals that affect both ourselves and the world around us. The more we concentrate on a thought, the stronger its frequency becomes, much like how a Tesla Coil amplifies electrical energy.

Simply put, thoughts are energy in motion. When directed with intention, they can shape reality, attract opportunities, and even alter the way we approach challenges. Tesla recognized the mind's immense potential—not just as a tool for thinking but as a conduit for energy capable of sparking innovation and creativity.

Key Concept: Focused Thought as Vibrational Energy

The more you focus on a thought, the more energy it accumulates. When you repeatedly concentrate on an idea, solution, or goal with intention, you are effectively "charging" that thought, making it more potent and capable of influencing your actions, decisions, and outcomes.

Brainwave Frequencies and Their Influence on Mental Clarity and Creativity

The human brain operates through electrical impulses known as brainwaves. These brainwaves are categorized into different frequency ranges, and each is associated with specific states of mind, emotions, and levels of consciousness. Here's a breakdown of the primary brainwave types and how they correlate with mental clarity, creativity, and thought energy:

1. **Delta Waves (0.5 to 4 Hz):**
   - Delta waves are the slowest brainwaves, primarily associated with deep, restorative sleep. They are essential for healing, regeneration, and physical rejuvenation.
   - During delta wave activity, the brain is less focused on external stimuli, allowing the body to undergo deep physical recovery.
   - Prolonged delta wave activity during waking hours is linked to sluggish thinking and lack of focus, but during sleep, it fosters the body's healing and repair.

2. **Theta Waves (4 to 8 Hz):**
   - Theta waves are prominent during deep relaxation, light sleep, and meditation. These frequencies are associated with creativity, sensory perception, and accessing the subconscious mind.
   - Research suggests that theta waves enhance problem-solving abilities and creativity by allowing the mind to explore connections between ideas that may not be obvious in a more conscious, alert state.
   - Studies on meditation have shown that experienced meditators exhibit increased theta wave activity, particularly in the prefrontal cortex, a region linked to creativity and innovation.

3. **Alpha Waves (8 to 12 Hz):**
   - Alpha waves occur when the brain is in a state of relaxed wakefulness, such as when you're daydreaming or in a "flow" state.
   - This frequency is known for promoting mental clarity, calmness, and heightened creativity. Alpha waves are common during creative activities, mindfulness, and light meditation.

TESLA'S CODE | 39

- o Research shows that alpha waves help reduce stress and anxiety, making it easier for individuals to tap into their creative potential and maintain emotional balance.

4. **Beta Waves (12 to 30 Hz):**
   - o Beta waves are dominant during periods of active thinking, concentration, and problem-solving. Higher beta frequencies are associated with logical thinking, focus, and productivity.
   - o However, excessive beta activity, especially in the higher range, can lead to stress, anxiety, and mental fatigue. Finding a balance between beta activity and the slower frequencies like alpha and theta is crucial for creativity and mental clarity.

5. **Gamma Waves (30 Hz and above):**
   - o Gamma waves are associated with high-level information processing, insight, and peak cognitive function. This frequency is often seen in moments of deep learning or heightened awareness.
   - o Recent research has linked gamma wave activity to states of "flow" and peak cognitive performance. Meditation practices, especially in advanced practitioners, can increase gamma wave production, correlating with higher levels of empathy, mental clarity, and perception.

Focused Thought and Brain Activity

Focused thought involves deliberately directing attention toward a specific idea, goal, or intention. This mental concentration not only impacts brainwave activity but can also physically alter the structure of the brain through **neuroplasticity**—the brain's ability to reorganize itself by forming new neural connections throughout life.

1. **Neuroplasticity and Focused Thought:**
   - Neuroplasticity allows the brain to adapt and change in response to repeated experiences, thoughts, or learning. By focusing on a thought or intention, neural pathways associated with that thought strengthen, making it easier for the brain to access and manifest related ideas or behaviors.
   - Studies on neuroplasticity show that sustained focus on a specific task or thought can reshape brain areas, such as increasing gray matter density in the hippocampus, which is crucial for memory and learning. The prefrontal cortex, responsible for executive function, also strengthens in response to focused thought, making individuals better problem-solvers and innovators.
   - For example, research by Dr. Richard Davidson has demonstrated that focused meditation practices can lead to lasting changes in the brain's structure, enhancing areas linked to attention, emotional regulation, and creative thinking.

The Impact of Meditation on Brainwaves

Meditative practices are known to alter brainwave patterns and improve cognitive function, mental clarity, and emotional well-being. Scientific studies on meditation offer insight into how this practice can help amplify thought energy and influence mental states.

1. **Meditation and Brainwave Activity:**
   - Theta and Alpha Waves: Numerous studies have shown that during meditation, particularly mindfulness or transcendental meditation, the brain

increases its production of theta and alpha waves. These slower frequencies help the mind relax, heighten creativity, and enhance access to the subconscious.

o Beta Waves: Meditation helps reduce the dominance of high beta wave activity (associated with stress and overthinking), leading to a more relaxed and focused state of mind.

o Gamma Waves: Advanced meditation practitioners, such as long-term monks or yogis, often exhibit increased gamma wave activity during deep meditation, correlating with heightened cognitive functions and deep emotional insights. Dr. Richard Davidson's research with Tibetan monks showed that their brains produced exceptionally high levels of gamma waves during meditation, far beyond the baseline seen in non-meditators.

2. **Scientific Support for Meditation:**

o Research by Sara Lazar at Harvard University has shown that meditation not only changes brainwave activity but also thickens the brain's gray matter, particularly in areas associated with attention, learning, and memory. Her studies suggest that meditation can slow age-related cognitive decline and improve overall brain function.

o Jon Kabat-Zinn, a pioneer in the field of mindfulness meditation, has shown that mindfulness-based stress reduction (MBSR) techniques can reduce the size of the amygdala, the brain's fear center, and increase the thickness of the prefrontal cortex, responsible for planning, decision-making, and regulating emotions.

Thought Energy and Manifestation

Tesla's idea that focused thought carries vibrational power and can influence reality finds some support in modern neuroscience and quantum physics.

- **The Observer Effect:** In quantum physics, the observer effect suggests that the act of observation can alter the outcome of a quantum experiment. This phenomenon parallels Tesla's belief that thoughts can shape reality by influencing energy at the quantum level.
- **The Law of Attraction and Thought Vibration:** While not entirely supported by mainstream science, the idea that thoughts carry vibrational energy and can attract similar frequencies is widely embraced in fields like energy medicine and metaphysical studies. Recent advances in epigenetics suggest that the way we think and feel can indeed influence the body at the cellular level, supporting the idea that thought energy can affect our physical reality.

Incorporating scientific research on brainwave frequencies, neuroplasticity, and the effects of meditation on brain activity into the section on **thought energy** will provide a more comprehensive understanding of how focused thought, much like Tesla believed, can be a powerful tool for creativity, problem-solving, and manifestation. These studies underscore that thought energy is not only metaphysical but has measurable effects on brain function and overall well-being.

Amplifying Thought Energy

Tesla's inventions often began as simple ideas. Through mental simulations and repeated visualization, he would amplify these ideas until they became fully formed solutions to complex problems. He treated his thoughts as vibrational currents, fine-tuning and amplifying them until they reached a frequency capable of influencing the physical world.

Similarly, you can amplify your own thought energy by focusing on your creative ideas, solutions, or goals with intention and repetition. The more energy you give to your thoughts, the more momentum they build, increasing their potential to manifest.

Exercise #9:
Amplifying Thought Energy Through Focus

1. **Choose a Thought or Goal:** Pick one idea, goal, or project that you want to bring to life. It could be an innovation, a personal objective, or a creative endeavor.
2. **Visualize the Thought in Detail:** Close your eyes and picture the thought or goal in as much detail as possible. Imagine how it will look, feel, and function once fully realized.
3. **Repeat and Amplify:** Over the next week, spend a few minutes each day focusing on this thought. Each time, add more detail and refinement. With each repetition, feel the thought gaining energy, becoming more vivid and powerful.
4. **Feel the Vibrational Shift:** As you continue this practice, notice how the thought or goal feels more real and attainable. You're not just thinking about it—you're charging it with energy, making it more likely to manifest in the physical world.

Thought Energy as a Manifestation Tool

Tesla didn't just believe that thoughts influenced the mind—he believed they could shape reality itself. In his view, thoughts were the building blocks of creation, vibrating at frequencies capable of bringing ideas into existence when harnessed properly.

This concept aligns with modern theories of manifestation, which suggest that when we focus on our goals with clarity and intention, we attract the resources, opportunities, and inspiration needed to bring them to life. By amplifying your thought energy and aligning it with your intentions, you become a powerful co-creator of your own reality.

Key Concept: Thought Energy as a Manifestation Tool

Manifestation happens when thought energy is focused, amplified, and aligned with action. It's not enough to simply think about what you want—you must charge that thought with enough energy and intention that it begins to influence your choices, actions, and the opportunities that come your way.

Tesla's Use of Mental Repetition

One of Tesla's greatest strengths was his ability to repeat and refine his thoughts over time. He would mentally simulate ideas again and again, each time adding more detail, energy, and precision until the thought evolved into a fully formed invention. This mental repetition not only amplified the power of his thoughts but also helped him troubleshoot potential problems before they arose in the real world.

You can apply the same technique to your own ideas and goals. The more often you think about a goal, refining it with each repetition, the more energy it accumulates and the more aligned you become with making it a reality.

Exercise #10: Tesla Coil Thought Amplification

1. **Pick a Project or Goal:** Select something you want to manifest or create. It could be a business venture, a creative project, or a personal goal.
2. **Visualize the Goal:** Spend a few minutes each day visualizing the goal in as much detail as possible. Imagine each step you'll need to take and the final outcome.
3. **Refine and Amplify:** As you continue to focus on the goal, refine it mentally. Add more details, improve your plan, and amplify the thought energy by repeating the visualization daily.
4. **Watch for Signs of Manifestation:** Over time, as the thought energy builds, pay attention to any signs that your goal is beginning to manifest. This could be new opportunities, insights, or resources that move you closer to your objective.

The Science of Vibrational Energy

Tesla's belief in the power of thought energy wasn't purely philosophical. His work with electricity, frequency, and vibration demonstrated that unseen forces could have a tangible impact on the physical world. He applied this understanding to his inventions, but he also saw it as a model for how the mind could influence reality.

Key Concept: Frequency and Vibration

In physics, frequency is the rate at which something vibrates. The higher the frequency, the more energy it contains. Tesla's inventions, such as the Tesla Coil, were designed to amplify and control frequencies to generate powerful results. Similarly, when you focus your thoughts on a specific frequency—such as a goal or idea—you are amplifying its energy, making it more likely to manifest.

Thought Energy as a Path to Innovation

Tesla's mastery of thought energy was central to his success as an innovator. He understood that thoughts were not passive—they were active forces, capable of shaping the world around us. By focusing on his ideas with precision, repeating them mentally, and amplifying their vibrational frequency, Tesla brought his visionary concepts to life.

As you practice harnessing your own thought energy, remember that the process is both creative and scientific. The more you focus on your ideas, the more energy they accumulate, and the more likely they are to manifest in the real world. By following Tesla's methods, you, too, can amplify your thoughts and use them as a powerful tool for creativity, innovation, and personal growth.

Exercise #11: Breathwork for Amplifying Thought Energy

Tesla believed that focused thought operates on vibrational frequencies capable of influencing both reality and the world around us. This exercise combines breath control with focused intention to amplify the vibrational energy of your thoughts and align them with your goals. Just as Tesla fine-tuned and amplified his thought energy to bring his ideas to life, this exercise will help you elevate and charge your thoughts with greater power.

Purpose: To amplify your thought energy by combining controlled breathing with focused intention, increasing the frequency and power of your thoughts.

Instructions:

1. **Find a Quiet Space**: Sit in a comfortable position where you can focus without distractions. Close your eyes and take a few deep breaths, centering yourself.
2. **Choose a Thought or Goal:** Select a specific thought, idea, or goal you want to amplify. It can be a creative project, a business goal, or even a personal intention.
3. **Begin Breathwork:**
   o Inhale slowly and deeply through your nose for a count of four, imagining that you are drawing in vibrant, energizing light.
   o Hold your breath for a count of four, letting that energy expand and charge within you.
   o Exhale slowly through your mouth for a count of four, releasing any doubts, fears, or distractions.

- Repeat this breathing cycle five times, focusing on building energy with each inhale and releasing resistance with each exhale.

4. **Focus on Your Thought:**
   - As you continue to breathe, bring your attention to the thought or goal you've chosen.
   - Visualize it clearly in your mind—what does it look like, feel like, and how will it manifest in your life?
   - With each inhale, imagine the thought becoming more vivid and powerful, charging with the energy you are drawing in.
   - With each exhale, release any doubts or fears that may block your thoughts from manifesting.

5. **Amplify the Energy:**
   - Continue focusing on the thought while maintaining breathwork. Imagine your thoughts glowing brighter with each breath, becoming more tangible and powerful.
   - Feel the energy

6. **Close the Practice:**
   - After 5–10 minutes of focused breathwork and visualization, slowly bring your awareness back to the present moment.
   - Take one final deep breath, and as you exhale, set the intention that your thoughts will continue to build energy and attract the right opportunities and solutions.

Goal: This exercise combines breathwork and focused thought energy to amplify the vibrational frequency of your ideas. By using your breath to charge and align your thoughts, you can increase their potency and create a powerful force for manifesting your goals, much like Tesla amplified his thoughts into reality.

In the next chapter, we will dive deeper into how thought energy interacts with the universal forces of vibration and frequency. You'll learn how to align your energy with these forces to create harmony, balance, and greater success in your personal and professional life.

Chapter 7

Aligning Thought Energy with Universal Vibration and Frequency

As we explored in the previous chapter, Nikola Tesla's understanding of thought energy extended beyond the mental realm—he believed that our thoughts, like electrical currents, vibrate at specific frequencies that can influence the material world. But Tesla's insight into energy didn't stop there. He recognized that to truly manifest creative ideas and achieve success, we must align our thought energy with the universal vibrations and frequencies that govern the cosmos.

In this chapter, we will explore how you can take Tesla's concept of thought energy to the next level by attuning it to the natural frequencies that exist all around us. By aligning your energy with these universal forces, you can enhance your ability to manifest your goals, create harmony in your life, and experience greater clarity in your creative endeavors.

Understanding Universal Vibration and Frequency

In physics, vibration refers to the oscillation of particles, while frequency is the rate at which something vibrates. Everything in the universe—from the smallest atom to the largest galaxy—vibrates at a specific frequency. This includes not only physical objects but also intangible elements like thoughts, emotions, and even consciousness.

Tesla believed that these universal vibrations form the foundation of reality. He often said, "If you want to understand the secrets of the universe, think in terms of energy, frequency, and vibration." He understood that by aligning ourselves with the natural rhythms of the universe, we could improve our mental, emotional, and physical states and manifest our desires more effectively.

Key Concept: Resonance with Universal Frequency

Resonance occurs when two objects vibrate at the same frequency. In the context of Tesla's ideas, resonance refers to the alignment of your personal energy—thoughts, emotions, and intentions—with the vibrational frequency of the universe. When you achieve resonance, you become a conduit for higher energy, amplifying your ability to create, innovate, and succeed.

The Science of Frequency and Its Connection to Thought

The concept that everything vibrates at a specific frequency is not just philosophical—it is rooted in science. For instance, the Schumann Resonance refers to the set of electromagnetic frequencies generated by lightning strikes and atmospheric conditions, often described as the "heartbeat" of the Earth. Research suggests that human brainwaves can synchronize with this frequency, creating a sense of harmony and well-being.

Tesla believed the human mind could do something similar. By aligning our thoughts with the natural frequencies of the Earth and cosmos, we can access higher states of creativity, problem-solving, and emotional balance. This alignment enhances mental clarity and allows us to "tune in" to the energy fields that shape the world around us.

Exercise #12:
Tuning Your Thoughts to Universal Frequency

1. **Find a Quiet Space:** Sit in a peaceful place where you won't be disturbed. Take several deep breaths to relax your body and mind.
2. **Visualize the Frequency of the Universe:** Close your eyes and imagine a subtle hum or vibration surrounding you, symbolizing the energy of the universe. Visualize this as a wave of energy moving harmoniously through everything around you.
3. **Align Your Thoughts:** Focus on a specific thought or goal you want to amplify. Imagine that thought vibrating at the same frequency as the universal energy. Feel your personal energy synchronizing with the broader energy field around you.
4. **Experience Resonance:** As you hold the thought, visualize it gaining strength and momentum. Picture it resonating with the universal frequency, growing in power as the two energies merge. Sense a feeling of clarity and connection as your thoughts align with the universe's vibration.

The Role of Emotions in Frequency Alignment

It's not only thoughts that carry vibrational frequencies—emotions do as well. Positive emotions such as joy, love, and gratitude vibrate at higher frequencies, while negative emotions like fear, anger, and despair resonate at lower frequencies. To fully align your thought energy with the universal frequency, it's essential to cultivate emotions that raise your vibration.

Tesla understood that maintaining a positive emotional state was critical to aligning with higher frequencies. He believed that emotions like curiosity, wonder, and passion for discovery were keys to accessing the creative forces of the universe.

Key Concept: Emotional Vibration

Your emotional state can either raise or lower your overall vibration, influencing the frequency of your thoughts and your ability to manifest desires. By fostering positive emotions, you create a resonance between your mind and the universal frequency, improving your ability to attract opportunities, insights, and solutions.

Using Frequency to Overcome Obstacles

Tesla's life wasn't free of challenges. From financial struggles to skepticism from the scientific community, he faced many obstacles that could have derailed his work. Nevertheless, Tesla stayed focused, driven by his belief in the power of frequency and energy to overcome adversity. He understood that by maintaining a high vibrational state, he could transcend the limitations of the physical world.

When you face challenges, it's easy to let fear, doubt, or frustration lower your vibrational frequency. However, by consciously choosing to elevate your thoughts and emotions, you can raise your frequency and align yourself with the flow of universal energy. This alignment allows you to access creative solutions, overcome obstacles, and remain connected to your long-term vision.

Exercise #13:
Raising Your Vibration to Overcome Challenges

1. **Identify a Challenge:** Think about a current obstacle or problem you're facing. How does this challenge make you feel? Acknowledge any negative emotions, such as fear, frustration, or doubt.
2. **Shift Your Focus:** Take a deep breath and focus on the positive aspects of your situation. What have you learned from this challenge? How can it help you grow? Cultivate feelings of gratitude for the lessons you're learning.
3. **Visualize Your Vibration Rising:** Picture your vibrational frequency increasing, aligning more with the universal energy. Visualize yourself overcoming the challenge with ease, guided by higher frequencies of thought and emotion.
4. **Resonate with Solutions:** As your frequency rises, concentrate on solutions rather than problems. Visualize the steps you'll take to overcome the obstacle and align yourself with the flow of universal energy, trusting that the answers will come.

Tapping into Higher Frequencies for Innovation

Tesla often spoke of tapping into a "universal knowledge" or "cosmic consciousness" to fuel his inventions and insights. He believed that by raising his frequency and aligning with the higher vibrations of the universe, he could access ideas and solutions beyond the reach of ordinary thought.

You can tap into this same higher frequency to fuel your own innovation and creativity. By aligning your thought energy with the vibrations of the cosmos, you open yourself to new perspectives, insights, and breakthroughs. This connection to universal energy allows you to think beyond conventional limits and access a deeper well of inspiration.

Key Concept: Innovation Through Frequency Alignment

Innovation comes from thinking beyond the ordinary. Aligning your thoughts with higher frequencies allows you to do just that. By resonating with universal energy, you can access creative ideas, solutions, and insights that feel as though they come from beyond yourself.

Becoming a Conduit for Universal Energy

Tesla's belief in the power of energy, vibration, and frequency was not merely theoretical—it was central to his work as an inventor, visionary, and problem-solver. He understood that by aligning his thoughts and emotions with the natural frequencies of the universe, he could amplify his creativity, overcome challenges, and achieve extraordinary results.

By following Tesla's example, you, too, can become a conduit for universal energy. Whether you're pursuing a creative project, working toward a personal goal, or solving a complex problem, aligning your thoughts and emotions with the higher frequencies of the universe will elevate your ability to innovate, create, and succeed.

Exercise #14:
Resonance Meditation for Frequency Alignment

Tesla understood that resonance—when two frequencies align—was key to harnessing the power of the universe. This meditation exercise will guide you through the process of aligning your personal vibration with the natural frequencies around you, allowing you to access higher levels of clarity, creativity, and harmony.

Purpose: To align your mind and body with universal frequencies, creating a resonance that enhances your ability to manifest goals and experience greater mental and emotional balance.

Instructions:

1. **Find a Comfortable Position:** Sit or lie down in a quiet, comfortable space where you can relax without interruption. Close your eyes and take several deep breaths, allowing your body to relax and your mind to calm.
2. **Visualize a Universal Frequency:** Imagine a soft, subtle vibration flowing around and through you. Picture this as a wave of energy—calm, steady, and infinite. This vibration represents the natural frequency of the universe, flowing in harmony with everything around you.
3. **Tune Your Body and Mind:** Focus on your breath as you inhale deeply. As you exhale, imagine your body and mind beginning to synchronize with the universal frequency. Feel your energy aligning with this larger, cosmic vibration. With each breath, your personal energy comes into greater harmony with the universe.

4. **Resonate with Universal Energy:** As you continue breathing, feel the resonance between your energy and the universal frequency. Visualize this connection growing stronger, amplifying your inner vibration and creating a sense of balance and peace.

5. **Hold an Intention or Thought:** Once you feel in sync with the universal energy, bring a thought, goal, or intention into your mind. Imagine this thought vibrating at the same frequency as the universe. Allow the resonance to amplify your intention, aligning it with the flow of the cosmos.

6. **Feel the Power of Alignment:** Spend a few minutes in this state of resonance, feeling your energy harmonizing with the universal frequency. Let go of any resistance, doubt, or negativity, allowing your thoughts and intentions to resonate with the higher vibrations around you.

7. **Gradually Close the Meditation:** After 10–15 minutes, slowly bring your awareness back to the present moment. Take a few final deep breaths, carrying the sense of harmony and alignment with you as you return to your daily life.

Goal: This meditation helps you align your personal vibration with the universal frequency, creating a powerful resonance that enhances your mental clarity, emotional balance, and ability to manifest goals. By regularly practicing resonance meditation, you can attune yourself to higher frequencies and access deeper levels of creativity and insight.

Chapter 8

Harnessing High Vibration for Mental Clarity and Well-Being

Throughout his life, Nikola Tesla demonstrated an extraordinary ability to maintain focus, clarity, and creativity, even under the most challenging circumstances. While his genius stemmed from intellectual brilliance, Tesla also understood the profound importance of energy and vibration in maintaining both mental and physical well-being. In this chapter, we'll explore how Tesla harnessed high vibrational energy to achieve mental clarity, manage stress, and maintain his health—and how you can apply these same principles to your own life.

The Link Between Vibration and Well-Being

Tesla believed that everything in the universe operates on vibrational frequencies, including the human body and mind. He recognized that when our personal energy is in harmony with the vibrations of the universe, we experience greater health, mental clarity, and emotional stability. Conversely, when our energy is out of sync—whether due to stress, overwhelm, or fatigue—our vibrational frequency lowers, often leading to mental fog, poor health, and a lack of creativity.

Maintaining a high vibrational state is essential not only for success in creative endeavors but also for overall well-being. Tesla understood that keeping his energy aligned with higher frequencies allowed him to perform at his peak, stay healthy, and tap into a continuous flow of inspiration.

Key Concept: High Vibrational Health

Health and well-being are directly connected to the vibrational frequency of the body and mind. Just as low-frequency states can lead to illness and mental fatigue, raising your vibration can enhance your physical health, emotional stability, and mental clarity. By cultivating high vibrational energy, you can create a state of optimal well-being that supports both your body and mind.

Tesla's Personal Practices for Mental Clarity and Energy

Tesla was known for his intense work ethic, often working long hours through the night. However, he was also keenly aware of the importance of maintaining mental clarity and energy. To ensure he could continue innovating and solving complex problems, Tesla adopted personal practices that helped him maintain a high vibrational state and mental focus.

1. **Solitude and Reflection:** Tesla frequently emphasized the importance of solitude in his creative process. He believed that quiet reflection allowed him to tune into higher frequencies and access deeper levels of insight and inspiration. By stepping away from distractions, Tesla could align his thoughts with universal energy and experience profound moments of clarity.
2. **Regular Walks in Nature:** Tesla believed in the rejuvenating power of nature. He often took long walks, especially at night, which he credited with helping him maintain a clear mind and gain bursts of inspiration. Nature's rhythms—whether the sound of a flowing river, the wind in the trees, or the hum of the Earth itself—have a calming,

grounding effect that helps align personal energy with the natural world's frequencies.

3. **Minimal Distractions and Simple Living:**
   Tesla lived a simple, almost ascetic life, free from unnecessary distractions. He recognized that a cluttered environment or excessive stimulation could disrupt his mental focus and lower his vibrational frequency. By maintaining simplicity and minimizing distractions, Tesla was able to sustain high levels of mental clarity and creativity.

Exercise #15:
Cultivating Mental Clarity Through Solitude

1. **Find a Quiet Space:** Set aside time each day to be alone in a quiet, distraction-free environment. This could be a room in your home, a peaceful corner in nature, or any space where you can reflect and recharge.
2. **Clear Your Mind:** Focus on your breath, allowing your thoughts to settle naturally. Don't force stillness; instead, let your mind quiet as you tune into your inner energy.
3. **Connect with Higher Frequencies:** Once your mind is calm, imagine tuning into a higher frequency of energy, just as Tesla did during his moments of solitude. Allow this elevated vibration to fill your mind, clearing away mental fog and inviting clarity.

The Science of Mental Clarity and Vibration

Recent research in neuroscience supports what Tesla intuitively understood—vibration and frequency play crucial roles in mental clarity and cognitive function. Brainwaves, the electrical patterns generated by the brain, operate at different frequencies depending on our state of mind. These brainwave frequencies—ranging from slow, restful delta waves to fast, focused beta waves—correspond to our levels of mental clarity, creativity, and stress.

Key Concept: Brainwave Frequencies and Mental Clarity

1. **Delta Waves (0.5–4 Hz):** Associated with deep sleep and rest, delta waves promote physical healing and rejuvenation. However, too much delta activity during waking hours can lead to mental sluggishness.
2. **Theta Waves (4–8 Hz):** Present during deep relaxation, meditation, and daydreaming, theta waves promote creativity, sensory perception, and access to deeper subconscious insights.
3. **Alpha Waves (8–12 Hz):** Alpha waves are linked to a relaxed yet alert state of mind, often present during reflection and creative flow. This frequency is ideal for mental clarity and problem-solving.
4. **Beta Waves (12–30 Hz):** These fast-moving waves occur during active thinking, focus, and problem-solving. While essential for productivity, too much beta activity can result in stress, anxiety, and burnout.

Tesla's ability to maintain a high vibrational state likely stemmed from his ability to balance these brainwave frequencies. By cultivating a state of relaxed alertness, he kept his mind open to new ideas while maintaining the focus necessary to bring those ideas to life.

Additionally, research has indicated that when individuals are exposed to environments that naturally resonate with the Schumann frequency, they experience enhanced cognitive function and emotional balance. Studies conducted by geophysicists and neuroscientists suggest that these electromagnetic frequencies help reset and synchronize our brainwaves, promoting a sense of well-being and reducing anxiety. This natural alignment with Earth's rhythm is believed to contribute to a harmonious state of mind, allowing us to access deeper levels of creativity and sensory perception, similar to what Tesla intuitively harnessed in his work.

On the other hand, disruptions in this natural resonance—due to artificial electromagnetic fields or stress—can negatively affect mental and emotional states, leading to increased agitation, confusion, or cognitive fatigue. Researchers in the field of neurofeedback have observed that training the brain to enter alpha or theta states through meditation or other focused practices helps mitigate these effects, restoring balance and mental clarity. These findings underscore Tesla's understanding of the importance of maintaining high-frequency mental states to access creative insights and sustain well-being.

By deliberately engaging in practices like meditation, breathwork, and mindfulness, we can amplify alpha and theta wave activity, aligning our brainwaves with the Earth's natural frequencies and achieving a heightened state of clarity, focus, and inner peace. This connection between brainwave states, the Schumann Resonance, and human consciousness provides a scientific foundation for Tesla's belief in the power of vibrational energy as a tool for mental and physical optimization.

Raising Your Vibrational Frequency for Optimal Health

Tesla understood that the body's vibrational frequency played a critical role in physical health, just as it did in mental clarity. He viewed the human body as a complex energy system and believed that illness could arise when the body's vibrational frequency was disrupted.

By raising your personal vibrational frequency, you can enhance both mental clarity and physical health. High-frequency energy promotes healing, reduces stress, and boosts your body's natural ability to restore balance.

Exercise #16:
Elevating Your Vibrational Frequency

1. **Focus on Positive Emotions:** Positive emotions such as gratitude, love, and joy vibrate at higher frequencies. Begin each day by focusing on these emotions, practicing gratitude journaling, or engaging in a daily meditation centered on love and appreciation.
   Engage with Nature: Like Tesla, spend time in nature to recharge your vibrational energy. Whether it's a walk in the park, listening to ocean waves, or feeling the warmth of the sun, nature's rhythms can help elevate your personal frequency.
2. **Mindful Movement:** Physical movement, especially when done mindfully, raises your vibration. Practices such as yoga, tai chi, or even simple stretching align your body's energy systems and foster a sense of well-being.

Maintaining High Vibration in Daily Life

Tesla's approach to living in high vibration was not a momentary practice but a daily commitment. By maintaining mental clarity, focusing on positive emotions, and staying in harmony with the universe's natural frequencies, Tesla was able to sustain a high level of energy and creativity throughout his life.

You can incorporate the same practices into your daily routine to achieve greater mental clarity, reduce stress, and enhance your overall well-being. By consistently raising your vibrational frequency, you align yourself with the flow of universal energy, unlocking your full creative potential.

Exercise #17:
Daily Vibration Alignment

1. **Morning Meditation:** Start each day with a short meditation focused on aligning your energy with the universe's frequency. Visualize yourself vibrating at a high frequency, harmonizing with the energy around you.
2. **Midday Reset:** Take a few moments during the day to reset your energy. Close your eyes, breathe deeply, and visualize tension or stress melting away. Realign your thoughts and emotions with positive, high-frequency energy.
3. **Evening Reflection:** Before bed, reflect on your day and identify moments when you felt aligned with high vibrational energy. Acknowledge any challenges and visualize yourself overcoming them with ease and grace.

Living in High Vibration

Tesla's ability to maintain mental clarity and well-being through his understanding of energy and vibration allowed him to perform at an extraordinary level throughout his life. By aligning his thoughts, emotions, and actions with the universe's higher frequencies, Tesla accessed profound creativity, overcame challenges, and maintained his health.

As you practice raising your vibrational frequency, remember that this is not a one-time effort but a lifelong commitment to living in harmony with the universe. By maintaining high vibration in your thoughts, emotions, and physical actions, you will experience greater mental clarity, emotional stability, and overall well-being.

In the next chapter, we will explore how to integrate these practices into your creative process, using high-vibrational energy not only for personal well-being but also to manifest your biggest goals and dreams. Just as Tesla used energy to fuel his inventions, you can harness this energy to create a life filled with purpose, innovation, and fulfillment.

Chapter 9

Using High Vibration Energy to Manifest Your Goals

In the previous chapters, we explored the concept of vibration and how Nikola Tesla harnessed high-frequency energy to maintain mental clarity, well-being, and creativity. Now, we turn our focus to using this powerful vibrational energy to manifest your goals. Tesla's ability to tap into the energy of the universe allowed him to bring groundbreaking inventions into reality, and you, too, can use high-vibration energy to manifest your desires, projects, and dreams.

In this chapter, we will explore how to align your thoughts, emotions, and actions with high-frequency energy to accelerate the process of manifestation, bringing your goals from the realm of thought into the material world.

The Power of Vibration in Manifestation

Tesla believed that everything in the universe vibrates at specific frequencies, and this includes thoughts, emotions, and intentions. Manifestation occurs when your thoughts and energy vibrate in harmony with the reality you seek to create. The energy you project through your thoughts and emotions shapes your external reality, attracting opportunities, resources, and outcomes that align with your vibrational frequency.

Recent studies in quantum physics, particularly the observer effect, suggest that the act of observation can influence the outcome of an experiment, lending scientific credence to Tesla's belief in the power of thought. The famous double-slit experiment, for example, demonstrates how subatomic particles behave differently when observed, shifting between particle and wave states based on the presence of a conscious observer. This phenomenon hints at a connection between human consciousness and the fabric of reality, suggesting that thought and intention may influence the material world on a fundamental level.

While the full implications of this quantum behavior are still being explored, these findings align with Tesla's belief that thought energy has the power to shape outcomes. Just as quantum particles respond to observation, it is possible that focused thought and intention can influence events in our lives. This intersection of quantum theory and human consciousness suggests that our thoughts, when directed with clarity and intention, may interact with unseen energy fields, creating real-world effects.

In addition, the emerging field of quantum biology explores how quantum phenomena might affect biological processes, including how our thoughts and emotions influence our physical bodies. Research into the mind-body connection reveals that intention and mental focus can alter brainwave patterns, physiological states, and even cellular activity. Tesla's view of thought energy as a creative force aligns with these insights, reinforcing the idea that our inner world of thoughts and intentions plays a crucial role in shaping the external reality we experience.

While quantum physics is still unraveling the mysteries of consciousness and its potential impact on reality, the parallels between these scientific discoveries and Tesla's pioneering ideas highlight the power of focused thought as a tool for manifesting goals. By harnessing the energy of our thoughts and aligning them with high-vibration frequencies, we may be able to influence the outcomes of our lives in profound and transformative ways.

Key Concept: Energy Follows Thought

One of Tesla's core beliefs was that thought is a form of energy, and where thought goes, energy flows. In other words, whatever you focus your thoughts and emotions on will naturally attract energy in that direction. If your thoughts and emotions are aligned with high vibration—such as positivity, confidence, and creativity—you attract experiences and opportunities that match that frequency. Conversely, low vibrational energy, like doubt, fear, or anxiety, blocks your ability to manifest your desires.

The key to successful manifestation is elevating your thoughts and emotions to a higher vibration, ensuring that your inner energy aligns with the reality you want to create.

How to Manifest with High Vibration Energy

To manifest your goals like Tesla, you must consciously raise your vibrational frequency and direct it with clarity toward your desired outcome. This process involves three main steps: setting a clear intention, aligning your energy with that intention, and taking inspired action.

A. **Setting a Clear Intention**

The first step in manifestation is setting a clear and specific intention. Tesla's success as an inventor came from his ability to envision his goals with precision. He could visualize his inventions in great detail, mentally constructing each part and running simulations in his mind before they were physically built.

Exercise #18: Clarifying Your Intention

1. **Choose a Goal:** Select a specific goal or project you want to manifest. Be clear about what you want to achieve, whether it's a personal goal, a creative project, or a career milestone.
2. **Visualize Your Desired Outcome:** Close your eyes and imagine your goal in vivid detail. See yourself achieving it. What does it look like? How does it feel? What impact does it have on your life or the world around you?
3. **Refine Your Vision:** The clearer your intention, the more power it has. Take the time to mentally refine your vision, adding as much detail as possible. The more specific you are, the easier it will be to align your energy with that vision.

B. Aligning Your Energy with Your Goal

Once your intention is clear, the next step is to align your thoughts, emotions, and actions with that goal. Tesla understood that the frequency of your thoughts and emotions directly influences the outcome of your efforts. If your goal vibrates at a high frequency—such as success, joy, or abundance—your energy must match that frequency.

Key Concept: Emotional Frequency

Emotions are powerful carriers of vibrational energy. Positive emotions like love, gratitude, and excitement vibrate at higher frequencies, while negative emotions like fear, doubt, and frustration vibrate at lower frequencies. By cultivating positive emotional states, you raise your overall vibration and bring yourself into alignment with your goal.

Exercise #19:
Emotional Frequency Shift

1. **Identify Emotional Blocks:** Reflect on any negative emotions that might be holding you back from manifesting your goal. Are you feeling doubt, fear, or anxiety about your ability to achieve it?
2. **Shift to Positive Emotions:** Consciously shift your emotional state to match the frequency of your goal. If your goal is related to abundance, cultivate feelings of gratitude for what you already have. If your goal is success, visualize yourself feeling confident and empowered as you take steps toward achieving it.
3. **Practice Daily Alignment:** Each day, spend a few minutes aligning your energy with the vibrational frequency of your goal. Focus on the emotions

associated with achieving your desired outcome, and imagine yourself already living that reality.

C. Taking Inspired Action

While setting an intention and aligning your energy are essential, manifestation also requires taking inspired action. Tesla was a master of mental visualization, but he didn't stop at visualizing—he acted on his ideas, bringing them into the physical world through hard work and determination.

Key Concept: Inspired Action

Inspired action flows naturally from your high-vibration state. It's not forced or driven by fear but guided by intuition and aligned with your goal. When you are in a state of high vibration, you will naturally feel drawn toward actions that support your manifestation.

Exercise #20:
Taking Inspired Action

1. **Listen to Your Intuition:** After aligning your energy with your goal, take time to listen to your intuition. What actions feel right? What steps can you take today to move closer to your desired outcome?
2. **Act on Positive Impulses:** When you feel the urge or nudge to take action, follow through. These impulses often come from your higher self, guiding you toward the path of least resistance.
3. **Be Consistent:** Tesla's success didn't happen overnight. He consistently took inspired action toward his goals, trusting that the energy he put into his work would manifest in the physical world. Stay

committed to your goal, taking one step at a time toward its realization.

Raising the Vibration of Your Environment

Another aspect of manifestation is creating an environment that supports high vibrational energy. Tesla surrounded himself with simplicity and avoided clutter, understanding that a chaotic environment can lower one's frequency and hinder creativity.

Exercise #21:
Vibration-Enhancing Environment

1. **Declutter Your Space:** Clear any physical clutter from your workspace or home. A clean, organized environment allows energy to flow freely, supporting mental clarity and vibrational alignment.
2. **Incorporate High-Vibration Elements:** Surround yourself with objects, colors, and sounds that raise your vibration. This could include plants, crystals, uplifting music, or items that bring you joy.
3. **Create a Sacred Space for Manifestation:** Designate a specific area in your home where you can focus on your manifestation practice. This could be a meditation corner, a vision board, or a journal dedicated to your goals. Use this space regularly to align your energy with your desired outcomes.

Tesla's Legacy: Manifesting Big Ideas

Tesla's ability to manifest groundbreaking inventions didn't come from luck—it came from his deep understanding of energy, vibration, and focus. He knew that the power of thought, aligned with high-frequency energy and guided by inspired action, could bring even the most ambitious ideas to life.

Just as Tesla envisioned wireless energy transmission long before the technology existed, you too can manifest your biggest ideas and dreams by aligning your energy with your goals. Manifestation is not limited to small, everyday desires—it can create life-changing outcomes and shape the future in ways you never imagined possible.

Exercise #22:
Visualization Amplification for Manifestation

Tesla used his vivid imagination to build his inventions mentally before they came to life in the physical world. This exercise will guide you in amplifying your vibrational energy through powerful visualization techniques that align your thoughts and emotions with the goal you seek to manifest.

Purpose: To enhance your ability to manifest goals by combining visualization with emotional and energetic alignment.

Instructions:

1. **Find a Quiet Space:** Sit in a comfortable, distraction-free environment where you can focus on your visualization. Close your eyes and take a few deep breaths to center yourself.
2. **Visualize Your Goal in Detail:** Imagine your goal as if it's already been achieved. See yourself living the reality you desire—whether it's completing a project, achieving a personal milestone, or launching a new idea. Visualize this in vivid detail, focusing on the sights, sounds, and feelings of having already manifested your goal.
3. **Amplify the Emotion:** Emotions are powerful amplifiers of vibrational energy. As you visualize your goal, focus on the emotions that come with it. Feel the joy, satisfaction, gratitude, or excitement of having achieved your desired outcome. The stronger the emotion, the more energy your visualization gains.
4. **Merge Thought and Emotion:** Imagine the energy of your thoughts and emotions merging together, creating a vibrant field of high-frequency energy.

Picture this energy growing and expanding, surrounding your entire being. As your vibrational frequency increases, feel your connection with the universe strengthening.

5. **Hold the Frequency:** Spend 5–10 minutes holding this powerful vibrational state, feeling your goal becoming more real and attainable. Imagine the universe responding to your elevated energy by aligning opportunities, resources, and people that will help you manifest your goal.

6. **Release and Trust:** When you're ready, slowly bring yourself back to the present moment. Release any attachment to the outcome, trusting that your elevated energy is already in motion, bringing your goal into reality.

Goal: This exercise helps you merge thought, emotion, and energy into a powerful manifestation tool. By regularly visualizing your goals with strong emotional alignment, you amplify your vibrational frequency and attract the resources and circumstances necessary to achieve your desires.

Becoming a Master of Manifestation

Manifesting your goals through high-vibration energy is both an art and a science. It requires clarity of intention, emotional alignment, and consistent action, but when done correctly, it can bring about profound transformation in your life. By applying Tesla's principles of energy and vibration, you can master manifestation, creating a life that reflects your highest vision and aspirations.

In the final chapters of this book, we will delve deeper into the long-term effects of living in high vibration and how to sustain this state as you continue to manifest your goals. By mastering these techniques, you will not only achieve personal success but also contribute to the evolution of human potential—just as Nikola Tesla did.

Chapter 10

Sustaining High Vibration for Long-Term Success

As you've learned throughout this book, raising your vibrational frequency is crucial for tapping into life force energy, enhancing creativity, and manifesting your goals. However, sustaining that high-vibration state over the long term is equally important. Nikola Tesla's ability to remain aligned with his visionary ideas and innovative thinking came from his consistent practice of staying in tune with higher frequencies of energy. To maintain long-term success, it's essential to keep your energy in harmony with your goals and continue evolving in both mind and spirit.

In this chapter, we will explore how to maintain high vibrational energy in daily life and how doing so can lead to sustained creative flow, personal well-being, and long-term success. You'll learn specific techniques to ensure that your energy remains elevated and in sync with your ambitions, just as Tesla stayed connected to the universe's vast reservoir of energy throughout his life.

The Challenge of Sustaining High Vibration

While it may be relatively easy to raise your vibrational frequency during moments of inspiration or when actively working toward a goal, sustaining that state day after day can be challenging. Life's inevitable stressors—whether related to work, relationships, or health—can pull you out of your high-vibration state and lower your energy frequency. When this happens, your ability to manifest and create with ease diminishes, and you may find yourself feeling blocked, frustrated, or out of alignment.

Tesla understood that the mind and body must remain in balance to continue functioning at a high level. He regularly engaged in practices that helped him maintain clarity, calm, and focus, allowing him to stay connected to higher frequencies of thought and energy.

Key Concept: Consistency in Vibration

The key to long-term success lies in maintaining consistency in your vibrational state. When you remain in a high-vibration mindset and environment over time, you build momentum that carries you forward, making it easier to attract opportunities, stay creative, and overcome challenges.

Daily Practices for Sustaining High Vibration

To sustain high-vibration energy, you need to incorporate regular practices into your life that keep you aligned with your goals and connected to positive energy. Here are some daily habits and rituals to help you maintain your vibration:

A. **Mindfulness and Meditation**

Mindfulness is the practice of staying present in the moment, while meditation is a tool for calming the mind and elevating your vibration. Tesla often used quiet contemplation and periods of reflection to maintain his clarity and connection to the energies around him.

Exercise #23:
Daily Meditation Practice

1. **Set Aside Time:** Choose a time each day for meditation—whether it's morning, midday, or evening—where you can be undisturbed for at least 10 to 15 minutes.
2. **Focus on Your Breath:** Begin by focusing on your breathing, allowing your mind to quiet and your body to relax. As you breathe deeply, visualize yourself surrounded by high-vibration energy, filling your body and elevating your frequency.
3. **Set Your Intention:** Use your meditation time to focus on an intention for the day or a goal you are working to manifest. Align your energy with that intention, raising your vibration to match the frequency of what you wish to attract.
4. **Ground and Center:** End your meditation by visualizing yourself grounded and centered, fully present and aligned with the high-vibration energy you've cultivated.

B. **Gratitude as a Daily Habit**

Gratitude is one of the most powerful tools for sustaining high-vibration energy. Tesla was known for his appreciation of the beauty and wonder of nature, often finding inspiration in the smallest details. By cultivating an attitude of gratitude, you continuously elevate your vibration and attract more positivity into your life.

Exercise #24:
Gratitude Journal

1. **Daily Gratitude Entries:** At the end of each day, take a few minutes to write down three to five things you are grateful for. These can be small moments of joy, achievements, or simple pleasures.
2. **Feel the Emotion of Gratitude:** As you write, allow yourself to feel genuine appreciation for each item on your list. The emotional frequency of gratitude naturally raises your vibration.
3. **Reflect on Your Progress:** Over time, look back at your journal entries to see how far you've come. This reflection helps reinforce the energy of abundance and keeps your focus on the positive aspects of your life.

C. Physical Movement and Energy Flow
Tesla believed in maintaining the health of the body as well as the mind. Physical movement helps circulate energy throughout the body, preventing stagnation and keeping your vibrational frequency high. Whether through exercise, yoga, or simple stretching, regular movement is essential for sustaining high energy levels.

Exercise #25: Morning Movement Routine

1. **Start with Stretching:** Upon waking, engage in a series of gentle stretches to wake up your body and get your energy flowing. Stretching helps release tension and boosts circulation, which elevates your energy.
2. **Incorporate Physical Exercise:** Choose a form of exercise that you enjoy, whether it's yoga, walking, or strength training. The goal is to move your body and stimulate the flow of energy.
3. **Focus on Breath and Intention:** While exercising, pay attention to your breathing and set an intention for the day. This keeps your mind connected to your goals while your body benefits from the movement.

D. Surround Yourself with High-Vibration
    Influences
    The environment you create around you can
    either support or hinder your efforts to sustain
    high-vibration energy. Tesla was known for his
    minimalist lifestyle, avoiding unnecessary
    distractions and clutter. He also valued the
    company of like-minded individuals who inspired
    him and shared his high-frequency vision for the
    future.

Exercise #26: Creating a High-Vibration Environment

1. **Declutter Your Space:** Remove any physical
    clutter from your environment that may be
    lowering your energy. A clean, organized space
    allows energy to flow more freely and supports
    mental clarity.
2. **Incorporate Natural Elements:** Bring elements
    of nature into your space, such as plants, crystals,
    or natural lighting. Nature vibrates at a high
    frequency and helps elevate the energy in your
    environment.
3. **Surround Yourself with Positive People:** Spend
    time with people who uplift and inspire you.
    Positive relationships reinforce your high-
    vibration state, while negative influences can drain
    your energy. Choose your company wisely.

Overcoming Energy Drains

Even with the best practices, there will be times when your vibration lowers due to stress, fatigue, or external challenges. The key to long-term success is recognizing when your energy is being drained and taking proactive steps to restore your high-frequency state.

Research in the field of psychoneuroimmunology has demonstrated that chronic stress and negative thought patterns can significantly weaken the immune system, making individuals more susceptible to illness and fatigue. Long-term stress triggers the release of cortisol and other stress hormones, which, over time, can impair the body's ability to fight off infections, regulate inflammation, and maintain optimal health. This directly impacts both physical and mental well-being, leading to burnout, anxiety, and even chronic health conditions.

Conversely, maintaining high-vibration emotional states—such as gratitude, love, joy, and compassion—has been shown to boost immune function, improve mental clarity, and increase overall resilience. Studies show that positive emotions activate the release of beneficial neuropeptides, which influence cell communication and strengthen the immune system. Dr. Candace Pert's groundbreaking research on neuropeptides, the chemical messengers that regulate emotions and bodily functions, reinforces this connection. Her work highlights how emotions directly influence our biology, with positive emotions leading to improved physical health and emotional balance.

This understanding aligns with Tesla's view that maintaining a high vibrational frequency is not only crucial for creativity and success but also for long-term health. Just as Tesla believed in the importance of mental clarity and emotional harmony, modern science confirms that cultivating high-vibration states can protect the body from the damaging effects of stress, enhance longevity, and support sustained personal growth.

By consciously fostering positive emotional states and managing stress through practices such as meditation, mindfulness, and gratitude, you can protect your body from the harmful effects of low vibration. This holistic approach ensures that both mind and body remain aligned with higher frequencies, supporting long-term health, resilience, and success in all areas of life.

Key Concept: Energy Management

Tesla understood the importance of managing energy, not just in his inventions but in his personal life as well. To sustain high vibration, you must become aware of what drains your energy and learn how to recover quickly.

Common Energy Drains:

- **Negative Thoughts and Emotions:** Dwelling on negative thoughts or emotions like fear, anger, or frustration lowers your vibration. When you catch yourself in a negative thought cycle, use techniques like mindfulness, meditation, or gratitude to shift your energy.
- **Toxic Relationships:** Interactions with people who consistently drain your energy can pull you out of your high-vibration state. Set healthy boundaries to protect your energy and choose relationships that uplift you.
- **Overwork and Burnout:** Working without breaks or pushing yourself too hard can deplete your energy reserves. Be mindful of your physical and mental limits and allow time for rest and recovery.

Recharging Your Energy

When you experience an energy dip, it's important to have strategies for recharging and realigning with your high-frequency state.

Exercise #27:
Energy Recharging Visualization

1. **Find a Quiet Space:** Sit or lie down in a quiet space where you won't be disturbed.
2. **Visualize Healing Light:** Close your eyes and visualize a bright, white light surrounding your body. Imagine this light infusing you with positive, high-frequency energy, restoring balance and vitality to every part of your being.
3. **Breathe Deeply:** As you visualize the light, breathe deeply and slowly, allowing each breath to fill you with renewed energy. Feel your body becoming lighter and more energized with each inhale.
4. **Set an Intention:** Once you feel recharged, set a clear intention for the rest of your day. Focus on maintaining your high-vibration energy as you move forward.

Tesla's Legacy of Sustained Innovation

Nikola Tesla's ability to maintain high-vibration energy throughout his life is one of the reasons he was able to continue innovating, even in the face of challenges and setbacks. His alignment with higher frequencies allowed him to stay connected to the universal flow of inspiration, enabling him to manifest ideas that were decades ahead of their time.

Exercise #28:
Body Scan

This exercise, originally designed for intuitive health awareness, can be adapted to help maintain a consistent high-vibration state by allowing you to check in with your body's energy flow daily.

Purpose: To enhance awareness of energy flow and release any blockages that lower your vibration, keeping your energy aligned for long-term success.

Instructions:

1. **Find a Quiet Space:** Sit or lie down in a comfortable, quiet place where you won't be disturbed. Close your eyes and take a few deep breaths.
2. **Scan Your Body:** Mentally scan your body from head to toe, paying attention to any areas of tension, discomfort, or low energy. Notice how different parts of your body feel without judgment.
3. **Release Energy Blocks:** As you scan, visualize any areas of discomfort being infused with healing, high-vibration energy. Imagine the

tension or blockages dissolving, replaced by
lightness and vitality.

4. **Align Your Energy:** Once you've scanned your
   body and cleared any blocks, focus on aligning
   your energy with the goal or intention for the day.
   Imagine your entire body vibrating at a higher
   frequency, fully in sync with the universe.

By incorporating these daily practices and energy-
management strategies, you, too, can sustain a high-
vibration state and remain aligned with your goals for the
long term. Whether you're pursuing a creative project, a
personal transformation, or a professional milestone,
maintaining consistent high-vibration energy will allow
you to achieve success with greater ease and flow.

Living a High-Vibration Life

Living a high-vibration life means more than just
achieving specific goals—it's about embracing a state of
being that allows you to flow with the energy of the
universe. When you consistently align yourself with
higher frequencies, you tap into an endless source of
creativity, inspiration, and personal power. Just as Tesla
lived in harmony with the energies of the cosmos, you,
too, can create a life that reflects your highest potential.

In the next chapter, we will explore how to integrate all
the principles you've learned into a lifelong practice,
ensuring that you continue to evolve, manifest, and
innovate in alignment with the highest vibrations of the
universe.

Chapter 11

Integrating Tesla's Code for Lifelong Success

In this chapter of this book, we bring together all the principles and techniques you've learned throughout your journey. From understanding life force energy to mastering visualization, amplifying thought energy, and sustaining high vibrational states, you now have a powerful toolkit for shaping your future and achieving lifelong success. This chapter focuses on how to fully integrate these teachings into your daily life so you can continue evolving and manifesting your highest potential—just as Nikola Tesla did.

The Journey Toward Mastery

Tesla's life was a testament to mastery—not only in the field of science and invention but in his understanding of energy, frequency, and the creative process. He didn't just develop skills; he lived them, embodying his understanding of the universe in every aspect of his work and life. His approach to life force energy, visualization, and innovation was not a series of disconnected ideas—it was a unified, holistic practice that allowed him to remain in constant alignment with his goals and the energies of the cosmos.

Key Concept: Integration

The journey toward mastery is about integration—
bringing all the principles and practices you've learned
into a cohesive way of life. You've already learned how to
tap into life force energy, use visualization to enhance
creativity and amplify your thoughts to manifest your
desires. Now, the key is to make these practices a natural
part of who you are.

Living Tesla's Code Daily

Tesla's genius was not only in his groundbreaking
inventions but also in his ability to remain deeply
connected to his inner world and the universal forces that
guide us all. To live Tesla's Code daily means to embody
the principles of energy, visualization, and thought power
consistently, aligning your life with the flow of the
universe. Here's how you can integrate Tesla's Code into
your daily life:

1. **Aligning with Life Force Energy**

Your connection to life force energy is the foundation of everything you do. When you are aligned with this energy, you experience vitality, creativity, and flow. Tesla understood that life force energy is not something abstract; it's a real, tangible force that permeates all things and can be harnessed for personal empowerment and success.

Exercise #29:
Morning Energy Alignment

1. **Start Your Day with Awareness:** Upon waking, spend a few minutes in quiet reflection. Breathe deeply and tune into your body, mind, and energy. How do you feel? What is your current vibrational state?
2. **Visualize Life Force Energy:** Imagine a stream of vibrant, high-frequency energy flowing into your body. See this energy filling every cell with light, vitality, and clarity.
3. **Set Your Intention for the Day:** Once you feel aligned with the life force energy, set a clear intention for the day. What do you want to achieve? What energy do you wish to carry with you? This practice helps you stay connected to life-force energy throughout the day, making it easier to maintain a high vibration.

2. Daily Visualization Practice

Visualization is one of the most powerful tools you have for manifesting your ideas, solving problems, and tapping into your inner creativity. By incorporating a daily visualization practice into your life, you can continue to refine your ability to see the future and make it a reality.

Exercise #30:
Evening Visualization

1. **Review Your Day:** At the end of the day, spend a few minutes reviewing what happened. What went well? What challenges did you face?
2. **Visualize Tomorrow's Success:** Close your eyes and visualize the next day unfolding. See yourself accomplishing your goals with ease, solving any challenges, and staying aligned with your highest potential. Picture the details—the people you'll interact with, the tasks you'll complete, and how it will all feel.
3. **Refine Your Vision:** If you encounter challenges during the day, use this time to mentally refine your approach. How can you improve? What adjustments can you make to ensure success? By visualizing your day in advance, you create a mental roadmap that aligns your energy and thoughts with positive outcomes.

3. Amplifying Thought Energy

Tesla understood that thoughts are not passive—they are active forces that shape reality. Every thought you have carries a vibrational frequency, and the more you focus on a thought, the stronger its frequency becomes. To live Tesla's Code means to actively direct your thoughts, focusing on those that align with your goals and avoiding those that diminish your vibration.

Exercise #31: Thought Energy Amplification

1. **Choose a Key Thought:** Select one thought or intention that is important to you—whether it's a personal goal, a professional aspiration, or a creative project.
2. **Amplify the Thought:** Close your eyes and focus on this thought with intensity. Visualize it as a vibrant, energetic force. See it growing in power and influence as you concentrate on it.
3. **Repeat with Intention:** Each day, return to this thought and amplify it further. The more you repeat and focus on the thought, the more energy it gathers, making it more likely to manifest in your life.

Maintaining High Vibration Over Time

Sustaining a high-vibration state over the long term requires conscious effort, but the rewards are immense. When you consistently maintain a high vibration, you remain open to inspiration, creativity, and opportunities that align with your highest potential. Tesla's ability to maintain his high-frequency state allowed him to remain innovative and visionary throughout his life.

Exercise #32:
Weekly Vibration Check-In

1. **Reflect on Your Week:** At the end of each week, take some time to reflect on your overall energy. Did you remain in a high-vibration state? Were there moments when your energy dipped? What caused these shifts?
2. **Identify Energy Drains:** Make a note of any activities, thoughts, or people that lowered your vibration during the week. What can you do to minimize or eliminate these energy drains going forward?
3. **Recommit to High Vibration Practices:** Review the practices that help you maintain a high-vibration state—whether it's meditation, gratitude, physical movement, or spending time in nature. Make a plan to incorporate these practices more consistently into your week.

Embracing Continuous Growth

Tesla's journey was one of continuous growth. He never stopped learning, experimenting, and expanding his understanding of the world. To integrate Tesla's Code into your life means embracing this same spirit of growth. The principles you've learned in this book are not static—they evolve as you evolve. Your understanding of energy, visualization, and thought power will deepen over time, and as it does, so will your ability to manifest, create, and innovate.

Key Concept: Lifelong Learning

Lifelong success requires a commitment to continuous learning and self-improvement. As you move forward, make it a habit to explore new ideas, experiment with different approaches, and remain curious about the world around you. Just as Tesla pushed the boundaries of what was possible, you, too, can expand your understanding of energy, creativity, and manifestation.

Your Journey Ahead

By embracing Tesla's Code, you have embarked on a transformative journey—one that connects you to the universal forces of energy and creativity that govern all of life. The principles of life force energy, visualization, thought amplification, and sustained high vibration are now part of your personal toolkit for success.

Remember, this is just the beginning. The journey ahead is one of constant evolution, discovery, and manifestation. As you continue to apply these teachings in your life, you will unlock deeper levels of creativity, insight, and innovation, just as Tesla did throughout his life.

Exercise #33:
The Tesla Manifestation Blueprint

As a final exercise, create your personal blueprint for manifesting success in the months and years ahead.

1. **Define Your Vision:** Write down your most important goal or vision for the next year. What do you want to manifest?
2. **Visualize the Process:** Close your eyes and visualize the steps required to achieve this vision. See yourself moving through each stage, overcoming challenges, and reaching your goal with clarity and focus.
3. **Amplify Your Thought Energy:** Focus on the thought of this vision daily. Use the techniques you've learned to amplify its energy and make it a powerful force in your life.
4. **Align with High Vibration:** Commit to maintaining a high-vibration state throughout the journey. Practice mindfulness, gratitude, and energy alignment to stay connected to your vision.

By following this blueprint, you are not only manifesting a specific goal—you are embracing Tesla's Code for lifelong success. The principles you've learned here will continue to support you as you grow, evolve, and achieve greatness in your own unique way.

As Tesla said, "If you want to find the secrets of the universe, think in terms of energy, frequency, and vibration." You now have the tools to unlock these codes and apply them to your life. The universe is waiting—go forth and create the future you've envisioned.

Chapter 12

Practice Is Key – Mastering High-Vibration Energy Through Repetition

One of the most important insights Nikola Tesla imparted to the world was that mastery—whether of technology, energy, or the mind—comes through consistent practice and focused repetition. Just as Tesla refined his inventions through mental simulations and meticulous adjustments, you, too, can achieve mastery over your energy and vibrational alignment through regular practice.

In this chapter, we'll explore why practice is the cornerstone of success in cultivating high-vibration energy and how repetition builds the foundation for long-term transformation. You'll learn that the true power of Tesla's techniques—and, indeed, of any energy practice—lies in consistency and perseverance.

The Power of Repetition in Energy Mastery

Tesla didn't reach his breakthroughs overnight. His success came from years of dedicated thought experiments, repeated visualization, and refining his ideas until they were ready to materialize. In the same way, raising your vibrational energy and aligning with universal frequencies requires dedication. Every time you engage in a high-vibration practice, you build momentum, raising your energy and sharpening your natural abilities.

Key Concept: Neuroplasticity and Energy Alignment

The brain's neuroplasticity—the ability to form new neural connections—works in tandem with vibrational energy practices. Just as repeated thoughts and actions reshape the brain, they also raise your vibrational frequency. Each time you visualize, meditate, or engage in exercises to elevate your energy, you're literally rewiring your brain and energy field to resonate at a higher level.

Repetition ensures that these new neural and energetic patterns become ingrained in your daily life, making it easier to stay in a high-vibration state even in challenging situations.

Why Daily Practice Matters

Consistency is key when it comes to energy work. While it's possible to experience powerful shifts during a single session of meditation, visualization, or breathwork, it's the cumulative effect of daily practice that leads to sustained transformation. Tesla understood this principle—he continuously refined his ideas and inventions over time, allowing each iteration to bring him closer to his desired outcome.

Benefits of Daily High-Vibration Practice:

1. **Increased Mental Clarity** – Regular practice sharpens your focus and enhances your ability to access creative insights quickly.
2. **Emotional Stability** – By repeatedly raising your vibrational frequency, you cultivate a baseline of emotional resilience, making it easier to manage stress and negativity.
3. **Enhanced Sensory Perception** – Intuition (gut instincts) is a skill that improves with practice. Daily energy work strengthens your connection to higher frequencies, allowing you to tap into intuitive guidance with greater ease.

4. **Manifestation Power –** Consistently aligning your thoughts, emotions, and energy with your goals accelerates the manifestation process, as your high-vibration state attracts the right opportunities and solutions.

Building Your High-Vibration Routine

To fully integrate Tesla's principles of energy, vibration, and manifestation into your life, it's essential to create a daily routine that supports your vibrational alignment. This routine doesn't need to be time-consuming, but it should be consistent and intentional.

Suggested Daily Routine:

1. **Morning Meditation (5–10 minutes):** Start your day with a short meditation focused on raising your vibration. Visualize yourself aligning with universal energy and setting an intention for the day.
2. **Gratitude Practice (3–5 minutes):** Take a few moments to reflect on what you are grateful for, shifting your energy into a state of appreciation and high vibration.
3. **Midday Energy Reset (2–3 minutes):** At some point during the day, take a quick break to breathe deeply, release tension, and refocus on positive energy. This helps maintain your vibration, especially during stressful moments.
4. **Evening Reflection (5 minutes):** Before bed, spend a few minutes reflecting on your day. Acknowledge any challenges and visualize how you overcame them with ease. Use this time to realign your energy for the next day.

Overcoming Resistance to Practice

Like any habit, there may be days when you feel unmotivated or distracted from your practice. Tesla faced countless obstacles in his life, but his unwavering commitment to his vision kept him moving forward. Similarly, maintaining your high-vibration practice requires dedication, especially when life gets challenging.

Tips for Staying Committed:

- **Start Small:** If you're feeling overwhelmed, start with just a few minutes of practice each day. Consistency is more important than length.
- **Track Your Progress:** Keep a journal of your experiences and any shifts in your energy, creativity, or emotional state. This will help you stay motivated as you see the positive effects of your practice.
- **Reward Yourself:** Celebrate your consistency. Every time you stick to your practice, acknowledge that you are building momentum toward greater alignment and success.
- **Find a Practice Buddy:** Share your journey with a friend or partner who is also working on raising their vibration. You can support each other in maintaining regular practice.

Practice Is the Path to Mastery

Just as Tesla continually refined his inventions through practice, your journey toward high-vibration living is one of ongoing refinement and evolution. Each time you engage in an energy-raising exercise or align your thoughts with higher frequencies, you are mastering the art of vibrational living.

Remember that the real power lies not in isolated bursts of effort but in the steady, consistent practice that allows your energy to transform over time. By embracing daily repetition and committing to your high-vibration routines, you are paving the way for long-term success, creativity, and personal fulfillment.

As you integrate these practices into your life, you will notice that living in harmony with the universe's highest frequencies becomes second nature, bringing with it a continuous flow of inspiration, well-being, and manifestation power.

Bonus Chapter

Advanced Practices for High-Vibration Living

As you've journeyed through the principles of energy, vibration, and manifestation inspired by Nikola Tesla, you've learned how to raise and sustain your vibrational energy to align with the universe's natural forces. In this special chapter, we delve deeper into advanced practices that will take your understanding and mastery of high-vibration living to the next level. These exercises are designed to sharpen your sensory perception, refine your thought energy, and deepen your alignment with higher frequencies.

These advanced techniques will enhance your mental clarity, creativity, and sensory perception, helping you stay in a high-vibration state for longer periods and manifest your most ambitious goals with greater ease.

Exercise #34.
Remote Viewing

Purpose: This advanced exercise sharpens your ability to mentally project yourself into the future, visualize outcomes, and access new insights. Remote viewing will help you tap into higher frequencies and gain clarity on long-term goals, opportunities, and challenges before they arise.

Instructions:

1. **Find a Quiet Space:** Sit in a comfortable, quiet place where you can relax and focus. Close your eyes and take a few deep breaths to clear your mind.
2. **Choose a Goal or Future Scenario:** Pick a long-term goal or a situation you want to explore. This could be a future project, a major life decision, or even the outcome of a challenge you're facing.
3. **Project Your Consciousness Forward:** Imagine mentally projecting yourself into the future, traveling forward in time to the moment when your goal or situation has been realized. Visualize yourself in this future scenario with as much detail as possible.
4. **Observe the Details:** Pay close attention to the details of your surroundings. What do you see, hear, and feel? How does the situation play out? Allow any intuitive insights to arise without forcing them.
5. **Gather Information:** Once you've visualized the outcome, mentally gather any important information that can guide you in the present. What steps did you take to reach this point? What challenges did you overcome?
6. **Return to the Present:** After exploring the future, slowly bring your consciousness back to the present moment. Take a few deep breaths and open your eyes, reflecting on the insights you gained.

Application: Use this exercise to gain clarity on the best course of action for long-term goals, whether personal or professional. It's particularly helpful when you need guidance on complex decisions or future outcomes.

Exercise #35
Automatic Writing

Purpose: Automatic writing taps into your subconscious mind, allowing higher vibrations and intuitive insights to flow freely. This practice helps unlock creative ideas and solutions, offering a way to channel your thoughts directly from higher energies.

Instructions:

1. **Prepare a Journal or Notebook:** Find a quiet, comfortable place where you can sit with your journal or notebook. Have a pen ready and set the intention to allow your higher self to guide your writing.
2. **Relax and Focus on Your Breath:** Close your eyes and take a few deep breaths, clearing your mind of distractions. Focus on your breathing to center yourself and open to higher energies.
3. **Set a Clear Intention:** Before you begin writing, mentally ask for guidance on a specific question, problem, or creative idea. Keep your intention clear but open-ended, allowing room for unexpected insights.
4. **Begin Writing Freely:** Without overthinking, begin writing whatever comes to mind. Don't worry about grammar, punctuation, or structure. Let the words flow naturally from your subconscious mind.
5. **Continue Until You Feel Complete:** Write continuously for 5-10 minutes, allowing your thoughts to pour onto the page. You may find that unexpected insights or new perspectives emerge as you write.
6. **Review Your Writing:** Once you've finished, read through what you've written. Reflect on any key themes, ideas, or solutions that stand out. These may offer new direction or clarity on your goal or situation.

Application: Use automatic writing whenever you feel blocked, stuck, or in need of creative inspiration. It's an excellent way to access your higher self and align with high-vibration energy for guidance.

Exercise #36
Thought Energy A –
Grounding Your Energy

Purpose: These exercises will help you understand how your thoughts and intentions shape your reality. By consciously directing your thought energy, you can align your mind with higher vibrations, influencing both your actions and the energy around you.

Instructions:

1. **Walk with Intention:** Go for a walk outside and imagine yourself deeply grounded, like a tree with strong roots. As you walk, feel the energy of the Earth supporting you, stabilizing your thoughts and grounding your energy.

2. **Notice Your Mental State:** Pay attention to how you feel during the walk. Do your thoughts feel calm, centered, and steady? Grounding your thought energy in this way helps align your mind with the Earth's natural rhythms, keeping your vibration steady.

3. **Reflect on Grounding:** After the walk, reflect on how the experience affected your thoughts and emotions. Did you feel more aligned and focused? This exercise helps you bring stability to your high-vibration energy, especially during stressful times.

Exercise #37
Thought Energy B –
Light as a Feather

Instructions:

1. **Walk with Lightness:** Go for another walk, but this time, imagine yourself as light as a feather, floating gently as you move. Allow your thoughts to feel expansive, free, and unrestricted by limitations.
2. **Sense Your Vibrational Shift:** As you walk, notice how your mental state shifts to one of lightness and possibility. Feel your vibration rising with each step, allowing creative thoughts to flow effortlessly.
3. **Reflect on Lightness:** After the walk, reflect on how this lightness affected your energy. Did you feel more open, creative, and inspired? This exercise helps elevate your vibration and expand your thought energy when you need to break free of mental barriers.

Exercise #38
Breath Exercise for Vibrational Clarity

Purpose: Conscious breathing raises your vibrational energy and helps you maintain mental clarity. This exercise connects breath with the intention to quickly elevate your vibrational state, making it an excellent tool for mental resets throughout the day.

Instructions:

1. **Focus on Deep Breaths:** Sit in a comfortable position and take three deep breaths, slowly inhaling through your nose and exhaling through your mouth.
2. **Set an Intention with Each Breath:** With each inhale, visualize yourself drawing in high-vibration energy. With each exhale, release any tension, doubt, or low-frequency thoughts.
3. **Amplify Your Energy:** Continue breathing deeply for a few minutes, each time focusing on raising your vibrational state with each breath. Feel yourself becoming lighter, clearer, and more in tune with universal energy.
4. **Seal the Vibration:** Once you feel your energy has shifted to a higher frequency, take one final deep breath and seal the feeling of clarity and alignment in your body and mind.

Application: Use this quick exercise whenever you feel mentally fatigued or when you need to reset your energy before a meeting, creative task, or meditation.

Mastering High-Vibration Practices

The advanced exercises in this chapter will allow you to deepen your connection to higher frequencies of energy, sharpening your sensory perception and refining your mental clarity. By mastering these techniques, you'll not only sustain your high-vibration state but also unlock new levels of creativity, personal power, and success.

These practices, rooted in both Tesla's understanding of energy and intuitive life principles, provide a toolkit for long-term vibrational alignment. As you continue to refine your awareness and mastery of energy, you'll find that living in harmony with higher frequencies becomes second nature, bringing both personal fulfillment and creative breakthroughs into every aspect of your life.

Appendices

Glossary of Terms

Acupuncture: An ancient Chinese medicine technique involving the insertion of needles into specific points on the body to balance the flow of Qi (vital energy) through pathways known as meridians.

Alternating Current (AC): A type of electrical current in which the direction of the flow of electrons switches back and forth at regular intervals or cycles. Tesla's development of the AC electricity supply system was one of his most significant contributions to modern electrical engineering.

Aura: An energy field believed to surround living beings, often perceived as layers of color, representing various aspects of an individual's physical, emotional, and spiritual health.

Bioelectromagnetic (BEM) Therapy: A form of alternative medicine that involves the use of electromagnetic fields to treat and heal various conditions, based on the premise that electromagnetic interventions can influence cellular and physiological processes.

Biofield: A term used in holistic medicine to describe a field of energy and information that surrounds and permeates the human body, playing a role in health and healing.

Chakras: According to ancient Indian medicine, these are energy centers within the body that help to regulate all its processes, from organ function to the immune system and emotions.

Craniosacral Therapy: A gentle, hands-on approach that releases tensions deep in the body to relieve pain and dysfunction, improving whole-body health and performance by manipulating the synarthrodial joints of the cranium.

Electromagnetic Field (EMF): Physical fields produced by electrically charged objects affect the behavior of charged objects in the vicinity of the field.

Energetic Hygiene: Practices aimed at cleansing, protecting, and balancing one's personal energy field or biofield. Examples include grounding, energy shielding, and regular meditation.

Energy Medicine: A branch of alternative medicine based on the belief that healers can channel healing energy into a patient and effect positive results.

Frequency: In the context of energy healing, it refers to the specific rate at which energy or vibrations oscillate or repeat.

Grounding (Earthing): The practice of connecting physically to the Earth's surface electrons by walking barefoot outside, which is believed to promote physiological and electrophysiological changes beneficial for health.

Hertz (Hz): The unit of frequency in the International System of Units (SI), which measures the number of cycles per second of any periodic phenomenon.

Kirlian Photography: A technique used to capture the phenomenon of electrical coronal discharges, often marketed as a way of visualizing a person's aura or biofield.

Meridians: In traditional Chinese medicine, these are invisible pathways in the body along which vital energy flows. Blockages or imbalances in this flow are thought to cause illness and disease.

Qi (Chi): In Chinese philosophy, it's the life force or vital energy that flows through all living things. It is the central underlying principle in Chinese traditional medicine and martial arts.

Quantum Healing: A holistic healing approach that draws on principles of quantum mechanics, suggesting that health can be restored through shifts in consciousness and the understanding that the body and mind are interconnected.

Reiki: A form of energy healing originating from Japan, involving the transfer of universal energy from the practitioner's palms to the patient to encourage emotional or physical healing.

Resonance: Tesla explored the concept of resonance in his experiments with electromagnetism. Resonance occurs when a system is able to store and easily transfer energy between two or more different storage modes (such as kinetic energy and potential energy in the case of a pendulum). This concept is relevant in energy medicine, where practitioners seek to bring the body's energetic systems into harmonic resonance for healing purposes.

Shamanic Healing: An ancient healing tradition based on the belief that a shaman (spiritual healer) can interact with the spirit world through altered states of consciousness to heal illness or restore balance to the soul.

Subtle Body: A term used in various esoteric traditions to describe a series of psycho-spiritual constituents of living beings, beyond the physical body, including the aura, chakras, and meridians.

Therapeutic Touch: A biofield therapy that involves the practitioner's hands being moved over the patient's body with the intention to detect and modulate imbalances in the patient's energy field.

Tesla Coil: An electrical resonant transformer circuit invented by Tesla. It is capable of producing high-voltage, low-current, high-frequency alternating-current electricity. Tesla coils are used in radio technology, and Tesla envisioned them as a way to wirelessly transmit electrical energy.

Vibrational Medicine: Healing practices are based on the idea that diseases can be diagnosed and treated by applying specific vibrational frequencies to the body, often involving sound, light, or magnetic fields.

Wireless Energy Transmission: Tesla experimented with the wireless transmission of electrical energy, demonstrating the potential to transmit electrical power without wires through the electromagnetic field. This concept of transmitting energy through the air has implications for thinking about the transfer of healing energy in biofield therapies.

Resources for Further Exploration

Books:

- "The Field: The Quest for the Secret Force of the Universe" by Lynne McTaggart
- "Energy Medicine: The Scientific Basis" by James L. Oschman
- "Hands of Light: A Guide to Healing Through the Human Energy Field" by Barbara Brennan

Websites:

- The International Center for Reiki Training (www.reiki.org)
- The Institute of Noetic Sciences (www.noetic.org)
- The Association for Comprehensive Energy Psychology (www.energypsych.org)

Journals:

- "Journal of Alternative and Complementary Medicine"
- "Evidence-Based Complementary and Alternative Medicine"

Conferences:

- Annual International Energy Psychology Conference
- Science and Nonduality Conference

How to Incorporate Energy Practices into Your Life

Daily Meditation and Mindfulness: Start or end your day with a meditation practice that focuses on visualizing or feeling energy flowing through and around your body.

Learn Reiki or Healing Touch: Many communities offer classes that can certify you in basic Reiki or Healing Touch, allowing you to practice these energy-healing techniques on yourself or others.

Practice Yoga or Tai Chi: These ancient practices combine physical movement with breathwork and energy awareness, helping to balance and enhance your body's energy flow.

Engage with Nature: Spend time in natural settings to connect with the Earth's energy. Grounding or earthing, such as walking barefoot on grass, can help realign your energy field with that of the Earth.

Explore Aromatherapy and Crystals: Incorporate essential oils and crystals that resonate with you into your daily routine, as these are believed to carry specific energy frequencies that can influence your biofield.

Seek Out Professional Energy Healers: For personalized guidance, consider consulting with practitioners of energy medicine to address specific health concerns or to deepen your understanding of your energy field.

By incorporating these practices and exploring the suggested resources, you can embark on a journey of self-discovery and healing, embracing the principles of energy medicine to enhance your well-being and connect more deeply with the world around you.

Scientific Appendix: The Science Behind Tesla's Code

In this appendix, we explore the scientific foundations that support Nikola Tesla's visionary ideas on energy, frequency, and the power of thought. For readers interested in the intersection of Tesla's metaphysical concepts and modern science, the following summaries of theories, studies, and research provide deeper insights into how Tesla's Code aligns with contemporary scientific understanding.

1. Brainwave Frequencies and Mental Clarity

- **Overview:** The human brain operates on different frequencies that correspond to various mental and emotional states. These frequencies can be measured as brainwaves, which are categorized as delta, theta, alpha, beta, and gamma waves. Tesla's intuitive understanding of energy and mental clarity correlates with our modern understanding of these brainwave states.
- **Key Studies and Theories:**
  - Delta Waves (0.5–4 Hz): Produced during deep sleep, delta waves promote physical healing, recovery, and immune function. These waves are essential for restoring energy and maintaining long-term health.
  - Theta Waves (4–8 Hz): Associated with creativity, sensory perception, and deep relaxation. Theta waves are prominent during meditation, daydreaming, and moments of inspiration, helping individuals access deeper subconscious insights.
  - Alpha Waves (8–12 Hz): Linked to relaxed focus, mental clarity, and problem-solving. Studies show that meditation and mindfulness practices increase alpha wave

activity, which enhances mental clarity and emotional balance. Neuroscientist Andrew Newberg's work highlights the impact of meditation on increasing alpha waves, fostering well-being and creativity.

o Beta Waves (12–30 Hz): These faster waves are associated with active thinking, concentration, and decision-making. Excessive beta wave activity, however, can lead to stress and anxiety if not balanced with restorative states.

2. The Schumann Resonance: Earth's Natural Frequency

- **Overview:** The Schumann Resonance refers to the natural electromagnetic frequency of the Earth, which averages around 7.83 Hz. This frequency is said to align with the brain's theta waves, which are connected to creativity, sensory perception, and healing.
- **Relevance to Tesla's Code:**
  o The Schumann Resonance has been studied in relation to how it affects human biology and mental states. Some research suggests that synchronization with this frequency can promote mental harmony, reduce stress, and enhance overall well-being.
  o Tesla's belief in the interconnectedness of the Earth's energies and human consciousness is reflected in modern studies that explore the effects of environmental frequencies on human health.

3. The Observer Effect in Quantum Physics

- **Overview:** The observer effect is a phenomenon in quantum mechanics where the act of observation alters the behavior of particles. This is best exemplified in the famous **double-slit experiment**, where particles behave differently when observed, suggesting that consciousness and observation may influence the physical world.

- **Key Studies and Theories:**
    o The Double-Slit Experiment: When particles pass through two slits, they behave like waves and create an interference pattern. However, when observed, they behave like particles, implying that observation changes their behavior. This aligns with Tesla's belief that thought energy can influence reality.
    o Quantum Consciousness Theories: Some researchers, including physicists such as John Wheeler and Amit Goswami, have explored the idea that consciousness plays a fundamental role in shaping reality. These ideas offer a scientific framework that supports Tesla's assertions about the power of focused thought and intention.

4. Psychoneuroimmunology: The Mind-Body Connection

- **Overview:** Psychoneuroimmunology is the study of how psychological factors, the nervous system, and the immune system interact. This field explores how emotions and mental states directly affect physical health, supporting Tesla's idea that high-vibrational states promote well-being.
- **Key Studies and Theories:**
    o Stress and Immune Function: Chronic stress releases cortisol, which suppresses the immune system and leads to increased susceptibility to illness. Research shows that positive emotions, such as gratitude and love, counteract the negative effects

of stress by promoting the release of beneficial neuropeptides.
- o Dr. Candace Pert's Research on Neuropeptides: Pert's work highlights the biochemical relationship between emotions and physical health. She discovered that neuropeptides, which transmit signals between the brain and the body, are influenced by emotional states, aligning with Tesla's view that maintaining positive emotional frequencies is key to health and success.

5. Neuroplasticity: The Brain's Ability to Change

- **Overview:** Neuroplasticity refers to the brain's capacity to reorganize itself by forming new neural connections in response to learning, experience, and focused thought. Tesla's mastery of mental simulation and thought energy mirrors modern understandings of how focused thought can physically alter the brain.
- Key Studies and Theories:
  - o Focused Thought and Brain Function: Research in neuroplasticity shows that repeated mental focus on a task or goal strengthens neural pathways related to that task. This concept is foundational to Tesla's belief that focused thought can manifest ideas into reality.
  - o The Work of Dr. Norman Doidge: In his research, Doidge explains how the brain can heal, adapt, and improve through mental training and focused intention. This scientific perspective aligns with Tesla's concept of refining ideas through repeated mental simulations.

6. Energy Medicine and Frequency Healing

- **Overview:** Energy medicine involves healing techniques that focus on manipulating the body's energy fields to promote physical and mental health. Tesla's work with electromagnetic fields and wireless energy transmission provides a framework for understanding modern energy healing practices.
- **Key Studies and Theories:**
  - Electromagnetic Therapy: Emerging research in the field of electromagnetic therapy shows that certain frequencies can stimulate healing processes in the body. Techniques such as pulsed electromagnetic field therapy (PEMF) are used to accelerate healing, reduce pain, and improve cellular function.
  - Frequency and Health: Research on vibrational medicine suggests that all living organisms emit vibrational frequencies and that imbalances in these frequencies can lead to illness. Tesla's understanding of frequency and vibration is mirrored in modern practices that aim to restore health by balancing the body's energy fields.

By examining Tesla's ideas through the lens of modern scientific research, we can see how his visionary understanding of energy, frequency, and thought aligns with cutting-edge discoveries in physics, neuroscience, and medicine. This appendix serves as a resource for readers who wish to delve deeper into the scientific underpinnings of Tesla's Code and how these principles can be applied to both personal growth and societal advancement.

Suggested Further Reading:

- "The Field" by Lynne McTaggart: A deep dive into quantum physics and the interconnectedness of all things.
- "The Brain That Changes Itself" by Dr. Norman Doidge: An exploration of neuroplasticity and the brain's ability to heal and transform.
- "Molecules of Emotion" by Dr. Candace Pert: A look at how emotions and neuropeptides interact to shape both mental and physical health.
- "The Holographic Universe" by Michael Talbot: A book that explores how quantum theories may explain paranormal phenomena and the nature of reality.

Bibliography

Tesla, Nikola

- My Inventions: The Autobiography of Nikola Tesla. [Original publication: 1919]
- Seifer, Marc J. Wizard: The Life and Times of Nikola Tesla: Biography of a Genius. Citadel Press, 1998.
- Cheney, Margaret. Tesla: Man Out of Time. Simon & Schuster, 2001.

Energy Medicine & Science

- Oschman, James L. Energy Medicine: The Scientific Basis. Elsevier Health Sciences, 2015.
- Becker, Robert O., and Selden, Gary. The Body Electric: Electromagnetism and the Foundation of Life. William Morrow Paperbacks, 1998.
- Oschman, James L. Energy Medicine in Therapeutics and Human Performance. Butterworth-Heinemann, 2003.
- Swanson, Claude. The Synchronized Universe: New Science of the Paranormal. Poseidia Press, 2003.
- BioInitiative Report: A Rationale for a Biologically based Public Exposure Standard for Electromagnetic Fields (ELF and RF). www.bioinitiative.org.

Quantum Physics & Consciousness

- Goswami, Amit. The Quantum Doctor: A Quantum Physicist Explains the Healing Power

of Integral Medicine. Hampton Roads Publishing, 2011.
- Radin, Dean. Entangled Minds: Extrasensory Experiences in a Quantum Reality. Paraview Pocket Books, 2006.
- McTaggart, Lynne. The Field: The Quest for the Secret Force of the Universe. HarperCollins, 2008.

Holistic Healing Practices

- Brennan, Barbara Ann. Light Emerging: The Journey of Personal Healing. Bantam, 1993.
- Eden, Donna, and Feinstein, David. Energy Medicine: Balancing Your Body's Energies for Optimal Health, Joy, and Vitality. TarcherPerigee, 2008.
- Myss, Caroline. Anatomy of the Spirit: The Seven Stages of Power and Healing. Harmony, 1996.
- Feinstein, David, and Eden, Donna. The Energies of Love: Invisible Keys to a Fulfilling Partnership. TarcherPerigee, 2014.

Integrative Medicine

- Weil, Andrew. Spontaneous Healing: How to Discover and Enhance Your Body's Natural Ability to Maintain and Heal Itself. Ballantine Books, 2000.
- Chopra, Deepak. Quantum Healing: Exploring the Frontiers of Mind/Body Medicine. Bantam, 2015.

Vibrational Medicine & Subtle Energy

- Dale, Cyndi. The Subtle Body: An Encyclopedia of Your Energetic Anatomy. Sounds True, 2009.
- Gerber, Richard. Vibrational Medicine: The #1 Handbook of Subtle-Energy Therapies. Bear & Company, 2001.

- Lipton, Bruce H. The Biology of Belief: Unleashing the Power of Consciousness, Matter & Miracles. Hay House, 2008.
- Sheldrake, Rupert. Science and Spiritual Practices: Transformative Experiences and Their Effects on Our Bodies, Brains, and Health. Counterpoint, 2017.

Energy Healing Modalities

- Miles, Patricia. Reiki: A Comprehensive Guide. TarcherPerigee, 2008.
- Hover-Kramer, Dorothea. Healing Touch: A Guidebook for Practitioners. Delmar Cengage Learning, 2002.
- Bradley, Fiona. Reiki for Life: The Complete Guide to Reiki Practice for Levels 1, 2 & 3. Piatkus, 2016.

Biophysics & Electromagnetism

- Polk, C., and Postow, E. (Eds.). Handbook of Biological Effects of Electromagnetic Fields. CRC Press, 1995.

Journals & Periodicals

- The Journal of Alternative and Complementary Medicine
- Evidence-Based Complementary and Alternative Medicine
- Global Advances in Health and Medicine
- Journal of Bodywork and Movement Therapies

Online Resources

- The Tesla Science Foundation: www.teslasciencefoundation.org
- The Institute of Noetic Sciences (IONS): www.noetic.org
- The HeartMath Institute: www.heartmath.org

- The International Society for the Study of Subtle Energies and Energy Medicine (ISSSEEM): www.issseem.org

Additional Scientific and Spiritual Perspectives

- Tiller, William A. Conscious Acts of Creation: The Emergence of a New Physics. Pavior, 2001.
- Kreiger, Dolores. The Therapeutic Touch: How to Use Your Hands to Help or to Heal. Prentice Hall, 1979.
- Srinivasan, T. M. Energy Medicine and the Human Biofield: A Practical Guide. Partridge Publishing, 2014.
- Dispenza, Joe. Becoming Supernatural: How Common People Are Doing the Uncommon. Hay House, 2017.

Acknowledgments

First and foremost, my deepest gratitude goes to Nikola Tesla, whose visionary work and untiring spirit continue to inspire the world. Tesla's groundbreaking innovations and ideas remain a powerful influence on this book, and his dream of harnessing energy for the betterment of humanity serves as a guiding light throughout these pages. Tesla's exploration of energy, frequency, and vibration is the foundation upon which this book is built, and his legacy is more relevant today than ever.

I would like to extend heartfelt thanks to the researchers, scientists, and practitioners who are advancing the field of energy medicine and pushing the boundaries of what is possible. Your dedication to uncovering the profound connections between science, consciousness, and healing has been invaluable to this work. The breakthroughs and insights you've contributed have enriched the landscape of energy medicine and continue to inspire new ways of thinking about health and wellness.

A special acknowledgment goes to my mentors and colleagues, whose wisdom, encouragement, and support have been pivotal in bringing this project to life. Writing a book that integrates Tesla's ideas with modern science and holistic healing practices has been a journey, and your guidance has been a constant source of strength and motivation.

To the Tesla Science Foundation, The Institute of Noetic Sciences, and similar organizations dedicated to preserving Tesla's legacy and advancing the exploration of energy, frequency, and consciousness—thank you. Your commitment to exploring the interconnectedness of science and spirituality has served as both a reference and an inspiration for the ideas presented in this book.

Gratitude is also owed to my editor, whose keen insights and unwavering patience have been instrumental in shaping this manuscript. Your feedback has not only improved this book but has also been a profound learning experience for me, one that I will carry forward in my future work.

I am deeply grateful to my family and friends for their continuous support, patience, and belief in my work. Writing this book has been a long and introspective process, and your encouragement has been a constant source of comfort during moments of challenge and doubt.

To the readers of *Tesla's Code: Mastering Energy, Frequency, and Creative Power,* thank you for embarking on this journey with me. I hope this book ignites in you the same curiosity and passion for discovery that has driven so many before us to explore the unseen forces that shape our world. May it serve as a guide to understanding the creative power within yourself and the energy that connects us all.

And finally, to the universe—for the subtle energies, endless mysteries, and the vast potential that exists within and around us—thank you. Your constant reminder that there is always more to discover keeps us reaching toward new horizons.

This book is a testament to the collective effort, inspiration, and shared vision of many. Together, we stand at the threshold of a new era in healing, guided by Tesla's legacy and the limitless possibilities that energy medicine offers.

With gratitude and excitement for the future,
Dr. Constance Santego

Message from the Author

Dear Readers,

With great excitement and a profound sense of purpose, I welcome you to *Tesla's Code: Mastering Energy, Frequency, and Creative Power*. This book represents the culmination of a journey that began with *Tesla and the Future of Energy Medicine*, followed by *Beyond Tesla: Advancing the Science of Energy Healing*. In this third volume, we dive even deeper into the realms of energy, frequency, and vibration, unlocking the secrets Tesla sought to reveal about the boundless power of creative energy.

Nikola Tesla's work, visionary as it was, offered glimpses into a universe where energy governs not only the material world but also the unseen forces that influence health, creativity, and consciousness. In *Tesla's Code*, we explore the essence of these forces, delving into how they can be harnessed for personal transformation, healing, and unlocking the full potential of the human spirit.

This book is a testament to the idea that Tesla's discoveries were not confined to the physical sciences but extended into the metaphysical realms of human potential. It is here, at the intersection of science, creativity, and spirituality, that the true power of Tesla's legacy comes to life. We explore how his work with energy and frequency offers us a roadmap to understanding the deeper layers of existence—ones that can shape our health, creativity, and, ultimately, our reality.

The goal of this book is to empower you. As you read these pages, I encourage you to see *Tesla's Code* as a theoretical framework and a practical guide. Through the techniques, exercises, and insights shared within, I hope to equip you with the tools to tap into your creative power, align with the frequencies that govern your life, and master the flow of energy that surrounds and permeates you.

Writing this book has been a journey of discovery, both personally and professionally. It has deepened my understanding of the profound connection between the scientific and the spiritual, the creative and the practical. In the process, I've realized that mastering energy is not about control but about harmony—learning to work with the natural forces of the universe to bring about healing, transformation, and creative breakthroughs.

As with my previous books, my vision extends beyond these pages. I hope that *Tesla's Code* will inspire you to explore, experiment, and expand your understanding of what is possible. Together, we can create a community of individuals dedicated to mastering their own energy and contributing to the collective well-being of humanity. I invite you to join me in continuing this journey through workshops, discussions, and an ever-growing network of like-minded explorers.

To the pioneers who continue to advance Tesla's legacy, to the energy healers, scientists, and visionaries pushing the boundaries of human potential, I offer my deepest gratitude. Your work and passion fuel the dreams of a future where energy and consciousness converge to create a new paradigm of healing and creativity.

And to you, dear readers, may this book inspire you to unlock the power within yourself, to live a life of resonance with the energies that shape our world, and to step into your own mastery of Tesla's code.

With infinite gratitude and enthusiasm,
Dr. Constance Santego

About the Author

Dr. Constance Santego is a visionary at the intersection of energy medicine, holistic healing, and modern science. With a background deeply rooted in both traditional wisdom and cutting-edge advancements, she has devoted her life to exploring the boundless potential of human healing and self-transformation. Dr. Santego's mission is to inspire others to reconnect with their innate power and unlock the extraordinary possibilities that lie within.

Holding a doctorate in Natural Medicine, Dr. Santego has dedicated herself to mastering a wide range of healing modalities, from Reiki Master and Educator to

Life Coach and Spiritual Mentor. Her passion for integrating the ancient with the modern is evident in her work, which spans the realms of energy medicine, spirituality, and personal empowerment. Whether through her teachings, healing sessions, or writing, she empowers individuals to embrace the full spectrum of their existence—physical, mental, emotional, and spiritual.

As the author of multiple books on energy medicine, Dr. Santego has gained recognition for her ability to translate complex concepts into practical tools for personal and professional growth. Her writings merge timeless wisdom with modern scientific principles, offering readers a roadmap to healing and empowerment. Each of her books invites readers to embark on a transformative journey of discovery, one where the lines between science and spirituality blur, revealing the limitless possibilities of healing through energy.

In *Tesla's Code: Mastering Energy, Frequency, and Creative Power*, Dr. Santego continues her exploration of Nikola Tesla's revolutionary ideas, merging them with the latest advancements in energy medicine and the science of human potential. This book, co-authored with ChatGPT, symbolizes a fusion of innovation and timeless insight, offering a comprehensive guide to tapping into the creative and healing power that lies within us all.

Dr. Santego's influence extends beyond her books. As the founder of a holistic health and wellness school, she has created a sanctuary for students seeking to learn the art of healing and to bring the wisdom of energy medicine to the world. Her school is a testament to her commitment to education, transformation, and the evolution of holistic health.

To learn more about Dr. Constance Santego's work, teachings, and journey, or to connect with her in workshops and discussions, visit www.constancesantego.ca. There, the paths of energy, healing, and creativity converge, offering the tools to transform your life.

Discover More

Embark on an Adventure with "Ikona – Discover Your Inner Genie"

Dive deeper into the world of empowerment and self-discovery with a range of offerings designed to inspire and transform. Explore the full spectrum of Constance Santego's motivational products, personalized coaching sessions, spiritual retreats, engaging live events, and enriching educational programs.

Connect, Learn, and Grow:

- Website: Journey further into our resources and offerings at www.ConstanceSantego.ca.
- Instagram: Join our community @Constance_Santego for daily inspiration and insights.
- Facebook: Stay updated with the latest events and connect with like-minded individuals on Constance Santego's Facebook Page.
- YouTube: Subscribe to Constance Santego's YouTube Channel for free resources, meditations, and more to guide you on your path to self-improvement.

Your journey toward personal growth and enlightenment is just a click away. Discover the tools and support you need to unlock your potential and manifest your dreams.

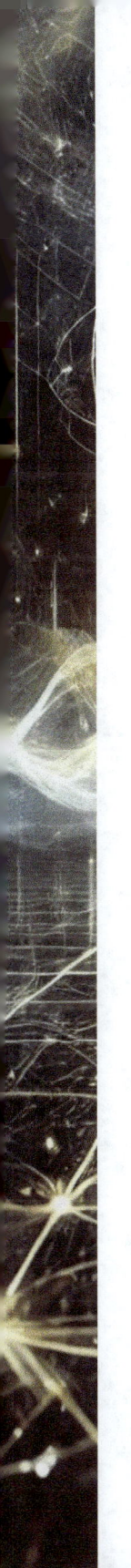

www.ingramcontent.com/pod-product-compliance
Lightning Source LLC
Chambersburg PA
CBHW071358120626
46546CB00002B/744